Elite E Services

4xv1
Forex, Version 1

2007

Elite E Services

Publishing information:

ISBN 978-1-4303-1133-1

Sunday, August 26, 2007

Published by:

Elite E Services

Corporate Offices

Elite E. Services Inc.

2620 Regatta Dr. Suite 102

Las Vegas, NV 89128

(702) 430-1629

Direct: (646) 837-0059

www.eliteeservices.net

email: info@eliteeservices.net

Distributed by: Lulu.com

4xv1

www.4xv1.com

Forex, Version 1 is the first version of a book about the foreign exchange market, from the perspective of the market itself: the computer. Think about it - what is the FX market but a bunch of numbers on the screen? Forex is nothing more than states of silicon, changing in real-time. See the forex market from the inside, from the perspective of the computer - as the market sees itself. www.4xv1.com

What you don't know about forex, and your broker can't tell you, and you can't learn in school.

Mark Markovic and Arthur Charloff have contributed to the intellectual content presented in this book.

This book is written by Joe Gelet, but by no means is he the real author. The information contained herein represents years of research and experience in the field, the author makes no claim to originality or copyright. The real author of this book is you, the consumer, who is driving global trade (and thus currency exchange) every time you go shopping, especially those of you who produce nothing and have a FICO score above 800. This book is dedicated to you, the consumer. If it were not for you, this system would not be possible.

Elite E Services www.eliteeservices.net

Purpose

This book was written to train and educate, enlighten and entertain. There is a lot of material floating around covering the same old things. There isn't a lot of insightful, groundbreaking work on what is going on in the forex market. Do many FX participants, and major players, really understand the dynamics of the forex market? FX is seen as an insignificant banking issue, yet if you consider how politics and FX are connected, and other factors explained here, the forex market is a revelation into the financial system itself. All markets are denominated in cash, at the end of the day. So, in some sense, forex is not a niche market but the most important financial engine in the world.

In this book, we review all aspects of 'the forex', from market dynamics, to trading strategies, lifestyles of the forex trader, and political implications.

Like many things in life, we can only open the door; it is yours to walk through. Take the blue pill, you can go back to your Money Market account and wait for inflation to eat you alive.

TABLE OF CONENTS

Chapters

Chapter 1: The Forex Market

Overview: The Currency Market

The foreign exchange market, or 'forex' market, is becoming increasingly popular in a wide variety of applications. Everyone knows that countries have currencies and they are traded against one another, but few realize the economic significance of these markets in their daily lives, and also there are many myths and rumors surrounding the forex market. In addition, few realize how to get involved in the forex market, and become discouraged when getting the wrong answers.

The forex market by nature is de-centralized because there is no official currency exchange such as for equities or commodities. On some exchanges, such as the CBOT, forex futures are traded as commodity contracts. However there is nothing stopping any bank from trading currency with another bank, with the CBOT, or with retail customers. There are no rules or regulations, and thus, there are many different opinions and packaging surrounding forex markets that are always disputed. The regulators in the US markets, such as the NFA, have stepped into take action involving forex trading, and provide limited rules to follow. It should be noted however that these regulators are involved only when you accept funds from the public. If you are a bank and have no customers, there are no regulations to follow regarding how to trade currency. The regulators are concerned only how you raise money from the public.

Forex strategy

Many people think that to trade currency you need to evaluate a countries economic performance, interest rate policy, and other macro-economic and geopolitical factors. While this no doubt influences the forex market, it is no longer the base of many traders' strategies. A new kind of trading is quickly evolving, based on mathematical analysis of prices, called indicators. If you have ever traded you are probably aware of common indicators such as RSI, MACD, Moving Averages, and Bollinger Bands. But programmers have expanded on this to create their own custom indicators, and some strategies monitor a plethora of indicators creating a super-indicator, which generates buy / sell signals. These strategies are very effective because traders can do an extensive amount of testing before trading live money on them. Finally, when live money is traded and it has a track record, the system can be easily replicated.

One popular platform, Meta Trader, allows anyone to download a demo version of their software which is 100% free. There are nearly 200 brokers in the world using this software platform, so if you find a technique which is working, you can open an account at one of these brokers and implement it with few problems. That means also that a programmer can code a strategy and use it at any of the brokers using Meta Trader platform. Strategies are compiled in files called "Expert Advisors" and can be implemented by clients without programmer or trader intervention. Due to the lack of restrictions and cost, there is a growing international community working on strategies for trading. Of course most of these people are amateurs, but not all of them. And in this case, being an amateur can be an advantage, because you have time to dedicate to the strategy (which requires a high degree of concentration) and possibly money to invest. Also you do not have rules imposed on you by a company or a market; it is a free development environment.

A further extension to these types of strategies and their implementation is seen in technology called Trade Robot. The robot collects buy / sell signals from hundreds of providers, and creates a signal database which includes auditing and tracking. After years of performance data, the robot knows what systems are profitable, and specific trade statistics such as length of trades typically seen by a system, and drawdown ratios. A drawdown is the calculation of loss when an account is losing. No strategy is perfect, even the best are subject to drawdowns, so when the sophisticated investor evaluates a system he is concerned less about absolute returns and more about drawdowns. For example if a system makes 200% with a 50% drawdown that means you are risking 50% of your capital to achieve a 200% return. Usually high yielding systems are very risky and have deep drawdowns, sometimes as much as 20% or more.

What is a pip?

In forex a pip is the smallest unit of measurement. In the EUR/USD 1 pip =$1 on a 10k contract. If the EUR/USD is 1.3448 the 8 represents 8 pips, if the EUR/USD moves from 1.3448 to 1.3449 that would be a 1 pip move. The value of 1 pip depends on the size of contract traded and the base currency, in this case USD. EUR/USD means that 1 Euro = 1.3448 USD. As this rate changes, your open position will have a profit or loss.

How does one get into forex?

Anyone who is new into forex should find someone in the profession who they can trust and can consult with. It is a small world and a trader likely knows a good broker and so on. We do not recommend investing a large amount of money into an account that you will trade, until you have learned the forex market well. There is no reason to drop your account by 50% as a learning curve – open a managed account. There are many successful forex managed programs that you can invest in while you learn. Then when you are ready to trade for yourself (if you want to) then open a mini-account for self-trading and leave money management to the pros. Of course there is a high degree of risk involved in any forex account, but in evaluating the best placement of the capital of a novice investor in the forex arena, it is best placed with someone with experience and track record.

Novice mistakes

If you are new to forex, there are many well produced educational courses you can take which will explain the details of forex trading and investing. However taking one of these courses will not make you an expert, nor will it give you the experience you need to trade as well or better than a seasoned veteran. It is recommended that while you are learning, you work with professionals who can guide you through initial stages of forex. If you don't want to know the details, that's fine too, but you should understand the nature of the market before even investing. Forex is a unique market and there are many features of forex investing that are not available in other markets, such as:

• You need only $1 to open a forex trading account at some brokers

• Many brokers will allow traders as much as 400:1 leverage, meaning with only $1,000 in your account you could trade up to $400,000 in currency!

• Forex is available in many shapes and sizes, there are few standards for trading and software

• The forex market is the most liquid in the world, with over $3 Trillion USD exchanged daily

Accounts and Brokers

A forex trading account is much like other types of accounts you may find at stock brokers or commodity brokers. Usually there are no commissions involved in forex trading, as brokers are compensated through the bid/ask spread. Although brokers offer tight spreads on forex contracts, as little as 3 pips on the EUR/USD for example, with large volume that can add up to substantial revenue for the broker.

11

A managed account is structurally the same as a self-traded account, except clients sign a Limited Power of Attorney giving a professional money manager access to trade their account. Traders have trading authority only, they cannot deposit and withdraw funds. The account is always in the name of the client, never give funds to a non-registered individual. Any professional would never accept client funds directly, funds are always handled by registered institution.

Common misconceptions

When you are investing in forex funds are not leaving the country! You are trading on the interbank market (or off-exchange market) in either case, brokers settle their aggregate positions end of day in a similar method to stock exchanges, debiting and crediting profit and loss to client accounts. It is not as if your funds are being 'wired' out of the country and back.

The forex markets are some of the most technologically sophisticated in the world due to their simplicity. In forex there are less issues relating to execution, auditing, and clearing, which enable the software to be designed small and simple. For trading for profit, or for designing automated trading systems, forex is clearly the superior market.

What is 'forex'?

Forex is short for foreign exchange (of currency). It can also be called FX or 4x. In a quick market you learn to talk quick.

Every country has a currency; a country *is* their currency. If you want to buy Maple Syrup from Canada, you need to pay in Canadian dollars, so the Maple Syrup maker can go buy the things he needs in Canada.

When a country sells its' goods and services, payment is eventually received in their local currency. If their goods are in high demand, there will be a short supply of their currency, as people will be willing to pay more and more, as it goes. Thus we have a free-floating currency system where countries trade their currencies based on trade value and also interest rates. Each holder of any dollars receives interest on that money, and the higher the interest the more attractive that currency is. Now think about the United States: during the 90's everyone in the world wanted to invest in the DOW, the NASDAQ, in small US-based businesses, and properties. Every single investor, before purchasing the above, needs to purchase US Dollars! Money flowing into the states can explain the strength of the dollar, in part.

The growth of the post World War 2 economy can be largely credited with the stable financial system put in place by F.D.R. called The Breton Woods Treaty. This laid out an economic policy for currency and exchange rates which were fixed, and that the U.S. would act as a world banker (all foreign central banks would hold U.S. dollars as a reserve currency), and the U.S. dollar would be backed by Gold and Silver[i]. In 1971 U.S. President Richard Nixon abandoned this agreement, and soon currencies began freely floating against each other based on market demands.

Now, it is possible for anyone with a computer to trade in the currency market. In a world of Globalization, where the largest U.S. retail distributor (Wal-Mart) imports its' goods from countries like China, currency investment combines all world financial markets. Americans, for example, may not understand that by NOT investing in currency they actually lost 50% since 2002, but they understand that gas is more expensive, along with many other imported products. Therefore an investment in forex is not a traditional 'investment' with the hope of potential return, it is a hedge against inflation caused by your local currency fluctuations.

A currency is a medium of exchange, a system of barter and economics. The currency is the system more significant than ideological philosophy, more than legal structure, more than the people. It is the benchmark to which all life, property, and prosperity is gauged.

Is it ironic that the currency market, driver of global trade and finance, without a doubt the most significant market in the world economy and politics, is the least known? Why is there such a void of information, and why are there so many misnomers regarding currency trading and investing?

From a traders perspective, the forex market is easier to trade in terms of execution and reporting, market hours (forex is 24/7), leverage (400:1), and ability to implement technical systems. There are only 8 major currency pairs, which have limited range, and are correlated mathematically.

In the stock market, the largest concern is insider trading. Insider trading is illegal in the stock market, because it is a specific unfair advantage that corporate officers have due to sensitive information they have. However, insider trading is not illegal in the currency market, because there are no 'insiders', and also it is not unethical for a bank to sell currency because that is the business of the bank! Insider trading does not apply to the currency market; in fact it is the least regulated market in the

13

world – because it is a money market. Currency traders are trading money for money, the highest form of trading. Every currency trade is determining the value of money.

At the bottom of the economic chain you have people who trade their manual labor for money. Then you have people who trade their goods for money, such as seen in futures and commodities markets. Finally you have those who trade pure information for money, which is information brokerage and some forms of Information Technology. Finally you have people who trade money for money, which is banking. Since we have abandoned the Breton Woods treaty and have a free floating currency exchange system, now another layer of complexity has been added, which is money being valued in terms of other money.

The reason for mentioning this is to illustrate that currency markets affect everyone. When the dollar is going down, it is decreasing in its purchasing power, creating inflation. This is not a commonly known mechanism because although the abandonment of Breton woods has completely changed our worldwide financial system, new books have not been written according to the new rules of the game. People think inflation comes naturally from the business cycle, when in fact it comes from the printing of money which creates oversupply. Now, with the new paradigm of money creation connected to forex trading, another element exists in the inflation equation that didn't exist before. Foreigners can buy your local currency and dry up supply. This motivates local central banks to print more currency to compensate and, thus we have a new inflationary paradigm of currencies each competing for their own destruction – the game is who can inflate more, quicker.

Especially in a world of globalization heavily dependent on global trade, specifically in the G8 and industrialized nations, the value of a countries currency exactly determines how many goods and services can be purchased and imported. Of course, if we can use our financial monopoly to decimate their currency and have more products for ourselves, all the better. International trade can take place by exchanging goods for goods – a sophisticated form of bartering. Or, we can manufacture money and purchase overseas goods backed by our banking system, which everyone is happy to accept so they can go out and purchase other goods from other countries (and a small % from us as well).

This delicate balance of financial power is demonstrated in the currency market, because of the mechanical procedure involved in remitting funds overseas. You need to exchange your

14

dollars for Euros, and when you do so you pay the price. Banks take no risk in the game and act as accountants for funds going back and forth from one currency to another.

Maybe a reason that there is little knowledge about forex is because the focus has always been on the mechanical aspect and not the economic impact. Maybe the financial establishment does not want to mention the fact that the reason the DOW is 13,000 is because the dollar is down, and a weak dollar is fuelling a real estate boom, and that real estate is just a gauge of inflation. Or maybe few understand the new paradigm of foreign exchange and the real value of money. Either way, there is little public information and understanding on the topic which is more significant than any other in modern finance.

Having said all of the above, you may wonder how to invest in such a market. There are basically 2 sides to the forex market; hedgers and speculators. Hedgers include any business or individual that is trading currency out of need – you sell your products overseas and require foreign currency or have multiple currencies budgeting in international markets. The second group (which is by far the minority) is speculators such as hedge funds and investment banks who take positions in the currency market with the hope for financial profit. The mechanism the speculators use to profit varies widely – from long term investment in a currency, to trading an automated 'day trading' system which takes many small trades in a day. There are also many strategies traders use that can become quite complex due to the mathematical relationship between currencies. For example there is triangular relationship between any 3 cross-pairs (for example EUR/USD, EUR/CHF, and USD/CHF). A trader may develop a strategy to capitalize on that relationship, or use it to 'hedge out' of a position by reducing his net exposure without taking on new positions. This type of strategy is unique to the forex market because of the cross pair system and the relationship between them. Other markets require derivatives to create such strategies (such as equity futures and options).

When investing in the currency market, one can find a professional trader who knows what he is doing, and evaluate the performance of different strategies and select one which matches his investment goals and risk profile. Some strategies are more risky than others, and there is a correlation between risk and reward. Many so called 'hedging systems' can work for months gaining as much as 50% per month, but always risk wiping out the account completely. Then there are more conservative strategies that may return 2% to 5% per month, less exciting but much less risky. Of course every strategy involves risk, there is no such strategy that is risk free in trading, and that is why no fund or trader can offer a guaranteed return. It is impossible to forecast a large amount of variables that could lead to losses.

No one is suggesting you shift your entire portfolio into fx - but a little education about the largest and most liquid market in the world, certainly wouldn't hurt any investor.[ii]

What do FCM's (brokers) do?

The retail FCM platforms you are familiar with are some of the most lucrative businesses in the world. They receive a price feed from the interbank forex market, and utilizing various custom software platforms, display the prices to retail customers. In the interbank market it is not possible to trade small amounts of money, so one service the FCM's do for their retail clients is bulking orders together, sending 1 large order directly into the interbank market instead of 100 small ones. They act as a point of contact for service, support, and usually have their own proprietary trading software which usually comes with news, charts, analysis, and sometimes other tools. They are compensated through the spread, which can be as tight as 3 pips and as wide as 15 pips on GBP/JPY.

Sometimes traders are called 'brokers' in other markets, because trades are executed by a broker (i.e. Stock Broker, Commodities Broker). In forex however the term 'broker' usually refers to the clearing house, in this case, the FCM. Forex traders are generally referred to as 'traders' (or in many cases 'pikers' if they experience pre-mature profit taking disorder) as forex is an OTC market a broker is not required.

The persons who are managing the order flow at the FCM are known as 'dealers'.

Beating the banks

Most people think that by virtue of the prices being offered in the retail platform that they are somehow 'beating the banks' - laughing at people in airports exchanging Euros to US Dollars at 300 pip wide spreads. You can't beat the banks, and besides, why would you want to? They are at the center of the interbank market, the only true market makers.

People think if there is a good trader, a good strategy, that outperforms others, well then the banks would be using it. If it's possible to make 20% per month or more in forex, the banks would be onto it. These people don't understand how banks work.

First of all, banks do not speculate in the forex market - why should they bear the risk? Banks want to have transactional profits of a penny multiplied by 10 million - small risk free profits with large volume. This way they can capitalize on their market position without risking anything.

Remember, the banks are your friends. Without them, FX would not exist. They are the heart of the market and the keeper of your funds.

Problem with banks booking profit

The banks are in the business of manufacturing money. A factory that manufactures chocolate, for example, would have a hard time paying their employees with chocolate. Many Americans had family members or friends who worked in the mid-west breweries in generations past, when beer was free, and they drank all day, and eventually had severe liver problems.

If bankers paid themselves billions in salaries, who would show up for work?

How do platforms make money?

Many platforms offer prices based on "no re-quotes" and "no slippage" and "our dealers don't trade against you".

Platforms have 1 goal in mind: volume. This is why they give you 100:1 or even 400:1 leverage. They are multiplying their profit 100 times. Consider you have a business selling hamburgers, but you have a side business as a bank. You loan your customers enough funds to buy 100 hamburgers instead of 1, creating 100 'virtual customers' that wouldn't otherwise exist. The customer pays back the loan immediately, which is secured by the value of the 100 hamburgers he now has. You just have to be sure that during the loan period he does not eat them, which is tracked by the platform software (if your account reaches 50% they will close your positions automatically). It's a no-risk way to increase their business size.

What you see in your retail platform is a total illusion. They may as well display pictures of Mickey Mouse or a thermometer going up and down. They want to cover their own positions that THEY receive from the interbank market. Contrary to popular belief, they are doing you a huge favor. One example is guaranteed fills. As much as clients complain about re-quotes and off-market prices, these traders would have a tough time scalping an Interbank platform for 10 pips.

Also there are many subtle ways brokers profit, which

most clients do not notice. If you have a USD based account for example, your profits always need to be converted back into USD once your position is closed. So if you take a non-USD based trade, such as EUR/GBP, you have a floating profit in GBP. But when you close your trade those GBPs will need to be converted into USD, so you really have 2 positions! However, brokers may charge 100 pip wide spreads on this exchange, because it will only equal a fraction of a percentage point of your total profit. If you take home $50.21 profit on a trade, you may not notice $.02 here or there. But it all adds up, multiplied by thousands of trades and thousands of clients.

There are banks which will hold large funds an extra day to collect an extra day's interest. Insurance companies will back their policies with Junk Bonds. By comparison to other financial institutions, the reputable retail forex brokers are clean as a whistle and quite mild in their profit making policies.

Retail FCM's are our friends

The retail platforms get a bad reputation without reason. They happen to be in a very precarious situation that most people don't think about. They do want you to make money, but they don't want angry clients to bring down the firm. 90% of the time, when a trader loses money, he blames the broker. At the end of the day, regardless of stops being taken, misquotes, it's over 10 pips here and there. If you're on the right side of the market, none of that should matter.

The retail platforms are actually doing retail clients a great service by delivering prices, and although they do occasionally (in individual cases) take advantage of their situation and position, they don't do this intentionally.

Anyone who complains about an extra 2 pips on a EUR/USD spread is not a serious trader. If you do 10 billion a month in FX volume, you will be getting a 1 point spread on the EUR/USD in an institutional platform.

Platform feeds are off

You can see price discrepancies between various platforms. Sometimes the lag is seconds, sometimes, up to a minute. This can be due to network connectivity, or large orders. Whatever is the cause, it can indicate where the price will go in the other platform.

Sometimes brokers will have different servers which could have differing price feeds. Open a demo account at your broker and run it next to your live account during NFP (Non-Farm Payroll) to see if they are playing games.

Belief Trading

A fiat currency like the US Dollar or Euro is ultimately a belief embedded in 'users' of the system. The USD is a system of barter and trade. Oil is priced in dollars hence the nickname "PetroDollar". Currency traders are really betting on market beliefs. Market participants consider interest rates, M3, the health of the economy, but ultimately investing in the USD is an investment in the 'dollar economic system', and a belief in the USD. When you sell USD and buy EUR you are betting on the Eurozone to beat the Dollarzone.

Base Currency of your account

For most retail accounts this is a no-brainer, you open your forex account in the base currency of your local economic region - if you are in United States you open a USD account, if you are in Germany you open a Euro account, and so forth.

Position example: If you have a base currency of USD and you take a position in EUR/GBP actually you have 2 positions! When you close your EUR/GBP position, you will have a profit in GBP which then needs to be converted into USD. In some platforms this 2nd position floats and is calculated based on a spot rate, and in others, you don't even see this happening.

The base currency is from an accounting standpoint where all FX positions are calculated from a Profit / Loss perspective. Ultimately all your positions will be converted to your base currency.

It's a small world after all

At the end of the day forex is an extremely small market in terms of market players. You have a short list of banks, a very small list of dealers who work for (or with) the banks, and then thousands of new participants due to the development of retail FCM platforms. 90% of the forex sites on the internet are white labels or affiliates of others. With 2 or 3 sources we end up seeing 20 or 30 companies, and it seems as if there are thousands of companies, when in fact most of them are the middleman.

Know your enemy

The banks are our friends, so are the FCM's, and your fellow traders are your friends, who is the enemy? The only enemy in forex trading is you. Only you get in the way of making money in the forex market. The only thing stopping you from success is your own disbeliefs and psychological issues. It's hard to accept, but trading is more a state of mind than intelligence or having the right tools. You need to have the right frame of mind and the right environment to trade. It varies person to person but trading is like meditating. When you dream, you should see your positions.

Do you really want to trade forex?

First you must ask yourself a very important question: Do you really want to be a forex trader? Forex trading requires strict discipline, the mind of a champion, access to large amounts of capital, and a significant time investment.

Anyone who tells you otherwise, simply, is lying. Forex trading is tough, risky, complex, and very few traders actually make money. This is NOT due to the previously mentioned FCM situation, because at the end of the day you are on the right or wrong side of the market. If you have what it takes, which primarily is the will and dedication, there is nothing stopping you from making millions or even billions. However once you go through the necessary learning curve to get that good, your values and concepts of money may change.

Skip the losses, open a managed

95% of all self-traded forex accounts blow out in the first 3 weeks. Whether you are just opening your first account, or are already frustrated with losses, consider a managed account. You wouldn't consider doing your own dental work; you leave it to the professionals. Trained or not, forex is more than a full-time commitment and you need to dedicate your life to trading. Anyone can make a great trader, but are you ready for that commitment? And if you are, can you beat the banks, years of systems development and testing, as offered by the current forex establishment? Why fight it? Try a managed account. Then at least you have someone's arm to twist.

If you have a desire to trade forex but don't want to risk your capital under your own trading abilities, open a standard managed account with 90% of your capital and trade 10% yourself with high risk / high leverage trades.

Make money in forex market without trading

You can cash in on the forex market without trading by participating in the business of forex industry. You can:

- introduce accounts
- invest in a manage account

- become an introducing broker
- focus on marketing rather than trading
- participate in the business side of forex

Everyone wants to be a trader, but no one wants to be a secretary. We all remember how the secretaries of Microsoft made out on their IPO. Being a desk jockey in this business means access to prime information in many cases. Also, there is a lot of profit to go around - and a lot of work to be done. If forex trading is not for you, find what is, and participate! We need accountants, lawyers, web designers, computer builders, real estate agents for our offices, etc. Find your niche if not as a trader - think of the market value of being a lawyer with saturated forex intelligence. Develop a reputation as a 'forex website designer' or for what your previous skill / profession is.

Be what you are, and still make money in forex.

Crosses explained

When you 'buy' EUR/USD you are entering into a spot exchange contract - you use available margin in your account (based in a base currency, usually USD) to secure the current price of that spot rate at that moment in time, speculating that it will increase or decrease. Technically speaking, by 'buying' EUR/USD you are long EUR and short USD.

Majors drag down minors

If there is a sell-off of the Euro it may be across the board - against everything. EUR/JPY, EUR/GBP, EUR/USD - may all be down. But some will be down more than others, depending on how the other crosses are doing. So for example if the pound is also weak, EUR/GBP may be down % wise less than EUR/USD because the dollar is strong and the pound is weak. You can make this interesting with a GBP/USD play as well.

EUR/USD then is a leading Euro indicator of what other Euro crosses are going to do. In some cases you can watch indications of a move in another cross - dealers start to hit the EUR/USD and it takes a few minutes for EUR/JPY to follow through. This is a good scalping technique as well as an indication of price action.

Introducing Brokers

An Introducing Broker or IB introduces new clients to FCM's and CTA's (firms and traders). He receives credit for the referral, but in many cases has negotiated a special deal (if you went directly to the firm you may not receive the same deal). To lure more clients to open accounts, IB's usually offer 'value added services' in addition to what you may receive by going to the broker directly. This can be in the form of software, services, signals, or cash rebates. There is nothing wrong with working with IB's in fact better you work with an IB than direct. In fact, the entire brokerage business is setup like a giant MLM pyramid, were inside a firm you have team leaders getting a % of lower employees like a 'down-line'. This motivates people to work unusually hard. IB's that are employed may have a very low base salary with high commissions, motivating them to produce for the firm.

There are 2 types of IB's, independent, and sponsored. If a firm sponsors an IB he can only introduce to that firm. Independent's have more freedom but usually receive less money and are less regulated due to their non-loyalty to any firm. Many firms have been built by the quality of their IB's and IB networks. Sometimes IB's may produce services and offer them through the main firm they are introducing too.

Stops

Don't use stops. If you enter a stop, you will probably get stopped out. Stops can be useful in complex strategies, or if you are going to be away from the computer (which is not recommended). If you really want to use a stop to protect your capital, use 'emergency stop' which is 150 points off the market.

"A stop is like having a 'kick-me' sign on your back" says one trader.

Also, some brokers will allow 'capital guarantee' that is, your account will stop trading if the fund level reaches -20% or whatever level you set.

Rollover Interest

Currencies bear interest of prime – discount. When you are trading in pairs, you either have to pay interest or you earn interest, depending on your position. For example if you are LONG NZD/JPY you are long New Zealand dollar and short the Japanese Yen. The NZD has an interest rate of 7%, and the JPY a rate of 0%. So by owning that pair (being long), you are paid 7% interest p.a. This is calculated daily, and hits your account at 5:00 pm EST. Some brokers, such as Oanda, do not use the Rollover system and pay Interest in real time. However Rollover is a common scheme used by many large retail brokers, so even if you are trading at Oanda you should be aware of this system. The fact that it is known to calculate at that time, it is possible to purchase a minute before 5 and sell a minute after to get the interest. You can see it marked on your account in real-time (see swap).

For Example, you can devise an entire strategy around traders who buy at 4:55 pm and sell at 5:01 pm. Definitely one should be aware of this, but unless you have a GBP/JPY position for 4 months, the rollover interest is small compared to the pip value of your trade. This is a classic trading 'what *not* to do' - trying to make $10 in rollover interest by risking $100 in pip value.

GBP/JPY

The most adored and feared cross in the markets; GBP/JPY can be approached by the experienced trader as a ticket out of forex trading. The British pound and Japanese Yen are both volatile currencies, subject to the whims of political turmoil (more so than other currencies), and less liquid than the AUD or USD. GBP/JPY is a nasty combination. Also used for a carry trade, as you are paid GBP/JPY interest. Since JPY interest is zero or near zero, and typically GBP has been higher than EUR or USD, GBP/JPY has been a classic carry trade cross.

Leverage

Leverage is designed that you can take multiple positions, not increase the size of a single position. This can mitigate your trade exposure instead of increasing it. For example you have a long EUR/USD position going south you can hedge your EUR/USD position with a EUR/JPY trade or a EUR/GBP short.

Triangulation

Pick 3 currencies and play the triangular cross:

EUR/USD - USD/CHF - EUR/CHF

You will see the relationship between 3 correlated crosses by watching their values in conjunction with each other. You will see a move in individual currencies reflected. For example, if there is a selloff in the EURO, EUR/USD will be sold, USD/CHF may not change or it will go up slightly, and EUR/CHF will be sold. Historically there has been 'triangular arb' (arb is short for arbitrage), when there is a discrepancy between the usual mathematical relationship (a selloff in EUR/USD which is NOT reflected properly in EUR/CHF). With the liquid markets and so many traders, it is rare to catch an arb opportunity like this. However, since currencies are traded in crosses and not individually, it is important to watch multiple cross rates of the same currency, especially 3 which are related such as above.

Lot Sizes

If you have a 100,000 in your account, use 10,000 lot sizes. Remember, you can always buy 10 lots which equal one standard lot. Always use the lowest possible allowed lot sizes. If trading 10 million, use 1 million lot sizes.

Single cross

Pick a currency you like and get to know it. Trade only GBP crosses or NZD crosses. Individual currencies have a trading pattern / style that you can pick up on only by focusing and following specific currencies for a long time. How does the NZD trade against the AUD, compared to how NZD trades against the EUR? During certain market hours?

Seasonal plays

When Germans have holiday they all go to Australia and New Zealand and take with them suitcases full of Euros, causing an artificial hump in EUR/NZD and EUR/AUD in the post January - February period. In march when they go back to work, they trade their NZD back to EUR and the cross re-adjusts. So say the Germans. But regardless, there are seasonal patters in currencies which can be played for the long term.

Like the harvests and weather affect commodity markets, seasonal factors effect the currency markets.

Refco Euro Sunday

"I made an average of 20 pips every Sunday for 12 consecutive Sundays going long EUR/USD with a 10 - 30 point take profit. One Sunday I made and then on the reversal as well. Refco ran the EUR up as much as 50 points before other players came in, and coincidentally, when Asia came in the EUR/USD was close to the opening price. Up and down, every Sunday. I never took any huge position, but what's wrong with an easy 20 pips to start the trading week off?"

- Find simple patterns and exploit them.

Tips

Remember, traders are just like you. Humans get tired, angry, excited, and so on. You are trading against other human beings, other traders. They are like you,

- Don't give into fear.

- Know when to stop trading and walk away – take a break.

- Be analytical, not emotional.

- Don't think you are smarter than everyone else. Listen to you fellow traders.

- Beware analysts who work for large houses promoting their own positions.

- Taking a $100 loss is better than allowing it to grow into $1,000.

20 Golden Trading Rules

Want to trade successfully? Just choose the good positions and avoid the bad ones. Poor trade selection takes a heavy toll as it bleeds your confidence and wallet. You face many crossroads during each market day. Without a system of discipline for your decision-making, impulse and emotion will undermine skills as you chase the wrong stocks at the worst times.

Many short-term players view trading as a form of gambling. Without planning or discipline, they throw money at the market. The occasional big score reinforces this easy money attitude but sets them up for ultimate failure. Without defensive rules, insiders easily feed off these losers and send them off to other hobbies.

Technical Analysis teaches traders to execute positions based on numbers, time and volume.This discipline forces traders to distance themselves from reckless gambling behavior. Through detached execution and solid risk management, short-term trading finally "works".

Markets echo similar patterns over and over again. The science of trend allows you to build systematic rules to play these repeating formations and avoid the chase:

1. Forget the news, remember the chart. You're not smart enough to know how news will affect price. The chart already knows the news is coming.
2. Buy the first pullback from a new high. Sell the first pullback from a new low. There's always a crowd that missed the first boat.
3. Buy at support, sell at resistance. Everyone sees the same thing and they're all just waiting to jump in the pool.
4. Short rallies not selloffs. When markets drop, shorts finally turn a profit and get ready to cover.
5. Don't buy up into a major moving average or sell down into one. See #3.
6. Don't chase momentum if you can't find the exit. Assume the market will reverse the minute you get in. If it's a long way to the door, you're in big trouble.

7. Exhaustion gaps get filled. Breakaway and continuation gaps don't. The old traders' wisdom is a lie. Trade in the direction of gap support whenever you can.

8. Trends test the point of last support/resistance. Enter here even if it hurts.

9. Trade with the TICK not against it. Don't be a hero. Go with the money flow.

10. If you have to look, it isn't there. Forget your college degree and trust your instincts.

11. Sell the second high, buy the second low. After sharp pullbacks, the first test of any high or low always runs into resistance. Look for the break on the third or fourth try.

12. The trend is your friend in the last hour. As volume cranks up at 3:00pm don't expect anyone to change the channel.

13. Avoid the open. They see YOU coming sucker

14. 1-2-3-Drop-Up. Look for downtrends to reverse after a top, two lower highs and a double bottom.

15. Bulls live above the 200 day, bears live below. Sellers eat up rallies below this key moving average line and buyers to come to the rescue above it.

16. Price has memory. What did price do the last time it hit a certain level? Chances are it will do it again.

17. Big volume kills moves. Climax blow-offs take both buyers and sellers out of the market and lead to sideways action.

18. Trends never turn on a dime. Reversals build slowly. The first sharp dip always finds buyers and the first sharp rise always finds sellers.

19. Bottoms take longer to form than tops. Fear acts more quickly than greed and causes stocks to drop from their own weight.

20. Beat the crowd in and out the door. You have to take their money before they take yours, period

Trading is a lifestyle

It would be quite insane for you to be trading forex while you are driving, for example. Trading should fit your lifestyle, and your lifestyle should be designed around trading. This can vary greatly depending on your character, style, upbrining, financial situation – so it is not appropriate to say it should be like this or that.   But it should have certain characteristics, which could be anything from high-rise office and corporate culture to a work-at-home mom trading Oanda while the kids are at school (better than watching Days of our Lives).

Forex = 24/7 Market

To trade forex you can forget your 9 - 5 plan. If you were a day-trader for example, you may have become used to the rhythm of waking up, having breakfast, and 2 hours of market action, followed by lunch and another 2 hours of action, and then the closing bell. This is not the case at all with forex. True, the forex market does include waves where the majority of the volume happens within a certain time frame, but it does not happen at exactly the same time every day. Gauging when the forex market will move is almost as difficult as gauging which direction it will move.

SMS Alerts are for lunatics

What kind of trader is drunk at a bar getting an SMS to buy EUR/USD and places an order on his celphone? It's even worse than stock quotes on your watch.

Guessing the volume is more difficult than guessing market direction.

Timing, timing, timing

Timing trades is more important than prices of trades.

Daily trading activity of the foreign exchange market.

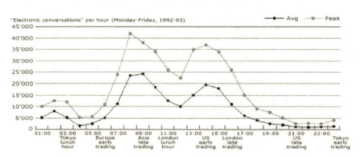

Note: Time value is Greenwich Mean Time (GMT).
Source: Reuters

Getting a good price is not nearly as important as getting in at the right time. Be willing to sacrifice 10 pips for the right moment. Not using this rule will get you stuck in low volume trades that last for way too many bars for your comfort, causing you to second guess the trades, and leave more possibility for error.

The quicker the trade, the better it is. Get in, get out, take the money and run. The longer you hold a position the higher the probability for a news event or large order to influence the market and change the direction. Holding positions = risk.

Volume and Market hours

The majority of forex trading happens 8:00 AM GMT, when the banks start to open in London and process last night's orders. Then it drops, and picks up when NY comes in.

Sometimes it is interesting to see what other regions do with the markets. Asians don't have deep pockets like NY and London and rarely create real market direction. However they are sometimes good for a strong reversal, and can sometimes tip the JPY enough to effect the USD or EUR at least technically, if not fundamentally.

Charting

Remember a chart is simply a visual historical representation of price action. The chart with the most information is the candlestick chart. The most reasonable time frame is the hourly. It should look something like this:

Time frames

Pick a combination of 3 time frames:

• short term (1 minute, 5 minute)
• medium term (30 minute, hourly, 4 hour)
• long term (daily, weekly)

Medium term should give you an overall snapshot of what the markets are doing this week. The short term is just an expanded medium term, giving you more precise price details (how did the market react during that news announcement). Long term charts are for long term trades, long term positions, 'investment' trades. For example when you are deciding what you want your base currency to be, you may look at the weekly chart or the daily. Since the inception of the euro it would have benefited euro denominated accounts.

Technical Analysis

Technicals can mean a lot in the forex market, not because of mathematical patterns, but because other markets can affect actual trades in the forex market. For example, Softbank may have a huge 10 billion option to buy EUR/USD at 1.1800 expiring at the end of the trading day. They may spend 1 billion in spot EUR/USD contracts to protect that 1.1800 level - the motive is there, but the question is always how deep are their pockets.

Demo Accounts?

Demo accounts are a great tool to see what forex is, how the software works, and it is always advisable to click a few trades through on the demo before going live. However, demo trading is not even close to the real thing. For some psychological reason, trading $250 USD in real dollars is different than trading $250,000 in fake money. Demos are great for learning software, but NOT as a benchmark for trading. Also, many platforms have demo servers that offer different prices than the real servers. That's because if the demo prices are off a few pips, they don't get complaints from angry traders!

Why is forex significant?

Many people scoff at forex as if it's another scheme to make money, as in the classic American style of multi-level marketing, or they think it's another day-trading fad which will pass with a big bust. The general public has become so distrustful with any well organized electronic capital market it seems. But junk e-commerce markets are touted as being the next electronic boon (Pay Pal, EBay, etc.).

Forex is significant because it is a market of money itself - the forex market determines the value of dollars - not in purchasing power - but in comparison to other dollars (such as Euros for example). From one perspective, all other markets are derivative markets, as they must be valued in some dollars. For example, you have an investment in GM stock; the stock price is PER DOLLAR. So while you are holding GM stock and the share price is fluctuating, so is the value of the US Dollar. Many people may not immediately notice this, because if the value of the USD goes down by 10%, it's not going to show up in your bank account as a loss. It's going to subtly show up as inflation, which may take months for you to realize, but it's going to hurt your pocketbook in the end. You will notice it at the gas pump, at the grocery store, and in the housing market.

Housing = Inflation

The housing market is really a gauge of inflation, so if you are making 20% per year on your house, you are only keeping up with inflation. It's not that the Fed is lying about inflation, it's miscalculated. I mean if housing is not a gauge of the value of money, what is then - gold? We have seen the gold price skyrocket - another signal that our money is becoming less and less valuable.

Money has never been so cheap.

Proof that we can all make money trading

A common misnomer in FX trading, as with any market, is the meme 'when someone is making someone else is losing'. This may be true with the stock market, but think about how FX is unique. We agree first it is possible for a large central bank to open an FX account at any broker, with anonymity, and deposit any amount of funds in that institution. That money could theoretically be wired out of thin air, created by the bank and sent to sit in an FX account at another bank. Then, they take huge positions randomly and lose 90% of their account. Did that money 'flow' into the hands of others? Or in other words, was that money pumped into the system through FX profits in other clients' accounts? If not, where did it go?

Lies & Myths dispelled

LIE: If someone had a profitable system in the forex market, they wouldn't share it with anyone.

If I have a system that makes 10% per month and I'm trading 100,000 - I can make 1000% more money if I trade 1,000,000 . Raising capital to the tune of 1M for forex trading is not as easy as one may think - large money is constantly being assaulted by systems developers about trading their systems. Large funds may look at hundreds of systems, and even after careful selection, it does not guarantee that the system will succeed in real time.

LIE: Forex trading is an easy way to make money.

A lot of people think forex is a way for easy money, when clearly that is not case. First of all, 95% of all forex accounts lose money. Secondly, there is an exact relationship between risk and reward, and like most people, who want the highest reward, they are willing to accept the highest risk. They only see the profit they don't see the potential for being wiped out. This works once in awhile, but it is certainly not prudent money management or is it a way to make money.

Myth: Bank of America profits by speculating in forex.

It is true that on their financials Bank of America lists 'foreign exchange' as a significant source of income. However this is misinterpreted by many as meaning Bank of America actually trades forex. They don't - this is purely transactional profit - they aren't SPECULATING in forex, they are a major player in the interbank market. For example if you have a savings account at Bank of America and you want to send 10,000 to Europe and you exchange your USD into Euros, they will quote you a 50 pip wide spread. This is where that profit comes from, NOT as if they have dealers speculating where the EUR/USD is going to be a year from now.

Myth: No one is making money in forex

There are many large, well known funds that have had horrible FX performance. That doesn't necessarily mean that everyone is losing. The thinking goes that if the big boys can't do it, no one can. But there are proven systems that are working. That doesn't mean they will continue to work, but it's not as if no one is making money in FX.

Chapter 2: Dynamics of the foreign exchange market

FX Politics

What is the purpose of FX?

Wouldn't it be great if we had a machine that just printed as much money as we wanted? Many claim the purpose of business = money. In other words, the final outcome of any business is profit or loss. The money is the results. So, the ultimate business, following that logic, would be to create a machine that just makes money! A golden donkey that shits gold. But then of course the problem is, if everyone had a golden donkey, who would cut your grass?

This is the game of central banks. Who can print more money, without letting on how much you are printing, is the winner. If the FED prints 500 billion this year, it should make the US Dollar slightly less valuable, to say the least. The problem with tin pot dictators is they all have the same idea: create a currency, and print as much money as you need to finance your wars. Again the problem remains that who accepts the money with your face on it, for supplies. If you've ever been to Walt Disney World, you have seen "Mickey Money" which you can use at any hotel, restaurant, or other venue inside Walt Disney World. But try giving Mickey Money to your telephone company when your phone bill is overdue and note the look on their face.

It is an elaborate poker game, who can bluff who the most. FX traders are the spread betters – you are betting on who has a better hand. You can bluff for so long, but in the end, your true hand is always revealed. This is why FX traders watch trade data. It's hard to lie about hard facts.

This is all known, and for this reason there always is a standard in finance, an all accepted standard such as gold. However, now the standard is the US Dollar. The dollar is the measure of which all other currencies are valued. Oil is traded mostly in USD, and it is the origin point.

Getting caught in the cookie jar

What is to stop FCM's from booking trades in house accounts that didn't exist? After the fact, a trade log could state that account 5464858 bought the EUR/USD at 1.2220 and sold at

1.2420 for a profit of $20 million dollars.

Is there a connection between money supply, liquidity, and FCM's? Does the fed pump money into the economy through FX market?

A trader of mine opened an FX account with $300 and traded for 2 weeks having a profit of over $3,000. Also, he generated $3,000 in rebates. Where did the $6,000 come from? He will take his profit and go in the real world and buy goods and services. My question is, where did the money come from? And, if it was conceived out of thin air, isn't it logical to assume that the financial establishment has figured this out for themselves too, and use it to their advantage? We will never know, although we do know the fastest growing consumer of US debt is offshore hedge funds in the Cayman Islands.

Campaign against FX

"FX Traders are a bunch of day-traders on steroids"

"If it's so great, why isn't everyone doing it?" – A valid question. Why not? Why is FX trading such a hidden gem?

Clearly there is a campaign, although not direct, to hide FX market from the investing and trading public. Surprisingly not even day traders have picked up on FX. Some even consider it like 'banking' or at least reserved for 'big banks'.

More than anything this is due to a lack of understanding. There isn't really any interest for a conspiracy against FX market like there would be for free energy for example. If FX becomes popular like day-trading did, every business can profit from it – there is not any day trading firm that can't easily offer FX services and cash in on the action. Why then, is there not more awareness about FX? Simply put, there exists a large lack of marketing. The opportunity in forex business in the next 5 years is in marketing, not trading. Now the FX community is mostly marketing to themselves and other competition, there is not much fresh meat.

Market is random – why no system can work all the time

Like any market, FX is managed by men. Like any men, they are subject to being emotional, angry, happy, excited, and jumpy. Those emotions can translate into trades, which can be substantial. Now, I do not mean to put them down as not being professional – they are trained like no other to mind supports and resistances, market forces, etc. But subconsciously, all these factors influence trade decisions.

Even automatically traded software can be influenced by humans – a trader can watch his account going down and shut off the software – where the next trade would have brought it back to profitability.

FX is not a capital raising, speculative market

Unlike capital markets, FX is an arm of the worldwide banking system. The EURO is not funded because investors are speculating that Europe is going to do well. However, European equities attract investment in Euros which does drive up the price of EUR/USD cross. So then what are FX traders doing when they are trading EUR/USD?

Derivatives run wild

Also, FX is what makes many derivative markets possible. An interesting one is interest rate swaps. The bearer of any currency supposedly bears the interest on that note – as banking customers with multiple deposit currencies will know, you get different interest depending on the dollars you hold. Knowing that central banks set rates and change them periodically, holders of notes can trade them for fixed or floating rates of others notes. This may seem complex, also to some it seems just like an accounting issue of big banks and big governments. But derivatives can be used in pension funds, for example, which can have disastrous effects on the economy. What if pricing models are incorrect, such as the case with LTCM. At the end of the day you don't have the funds to clear your transactions – it means somewhere down the line someone isn't getting paid. This can cause a run on the banks or problems with financial institutions themselves. In today's world this seems uncommon like it may have been in the 20's or 30's – yet there are hundreds of millions of dollars frozen at Refco. Billions were frozen in the Balkan wars in the 90's, and certainly we have seen huge companies fall due to accounting issues. Everyone assumes fraud and is quick to ring the neck of apparently crooked CEO's – what they are NOT willing to accept, is that the system is breaking down. The clear answer is right in front of everyone's nose: the problems with WorldCom and Enron, etc. are not moral they are systemic – our system cannot grow and cannot sustain itself in its present form.

FX is going to be brought down

This (FX trading) is really a big waste of our time. A number of things can happen to the system, but one thing will happen to FX for sure: the game will end. One way or another, this is a short lived racket that can have a number of possible outcomes:

- 1 world currency

- FX consolidates into 2 or 3 regional currencies such as the EURO there is the ASIO and the USD eates up the Mexican Peso, CAD, and all of South America

- a new gold backed reserve currency is used as a new digital cash to which all currencies are pegged (against it, but are still floating against each other)

FX market as we know it, the floating system, was created on a whim by Richard Nixon who didn't have enough gold to pay the French who demanded full upfront payment as outlined in Breton Woods. It can just as easily be destroyed (as we know it) on a whim, caused by some global conflict, natural disaster, geopolitical turmoil, who knows. What is certain is that it will not last forever, a new paradigm of money will emerge in this age.

No one is an absolute authority on FX

Similar to the way the FX market is transacted, via a network of unconnected 'interbank' markets (unlike a centralized market such as a stock exchange), so is power and knowledge about the FX market.

For example, a company is running a fully automated black box trading arbitrage system taking advantage of various feeds' small price discrepancies. They run the system for months, making huge profits at the expense of the feed providers. They find out, and begin throwing bad prices off to throw off the arb system. There are no rules against placing and removing bids, it's an open market.

But this went on without the knowledge of 'most' in the FX community, thus if you were to ask influential or knowledgeable FX traders they may have denied the existence of such a system. Therefore, how is it even possible for one to collect information in this environment?

Fast paced information curve

By the time this book is printed, it's already out of date. That's why the format of an updateable e-book was chosen as the primary source. There are things that will happen in this market that only few now know. And collecting all the information is impossible due to the time/information curve moving so quickly. By the time you collect all the info, it has changed.

If you are running a major FX company, do you have time

to read a 50 page report detailing how the FX market is rigged? But on the other hand, you may be out there in the real world making history while analysts are discussing something they think you are doing when in reality you are working on another project altogether. Making an exact picture is impossible, and in this case the business dealings of FX firms and traders are directly connected to the FX market, as their accounts, decisions, and psychology, all play into how the market trades, as well as the systems that are executing orders – especially automated systems.

FX Drives Immigration

Where is the strong dollar, you find waves of immigrants wanting to work and trade for those strong dollars.

FX Rhythm of life markets

FX markets seem to ebb and flow with the global collective subconscious. FX markets do NOT 'open' and 'close' – so why do markets move at times like 8:00 am? Because traders have a market open time burned into their brain. Because there is proven, scientific evidence that human thought can affect a random number generator. It's why you can sense a busy office – or a quiet pasture. Everyone can feel other people's thoughts, even if you're not psychic. That's why we love a good rock concert – concentrated energy. We are all focused on 1 thing – having a good time. It's also why the million man march can easily turn into a revolution. Millions of stomping people all mad because the president, or the king, has wronged them.

Have you ever been in a trade, and your girlfriend or wife happens to call, just as the market is moving? It's not bad luck; it couldn't be any other way. In other words, the forces that cause the market to move are the same forces that cause her to call. Maybe another wife called a trader at a big bank, which caused him to prematurely press the 'sell' key instead of waiting 20 minutes as he was instructed. Don't forget at the end of the day, markets are run by humans, not computers.

The global consciousness project

Every trader should explore this project, as it has severe implications for the markets. Not digging too deep into any pseudo science, use it as a hyperbole for how markets operate. Staring at the number generators is much like staring at a bunch of cross rates without charts. Like the matrix, and like life, you start to see patterns and a woman in a red dress. Stare long enough, and you can see what will happen next. [iii]

36

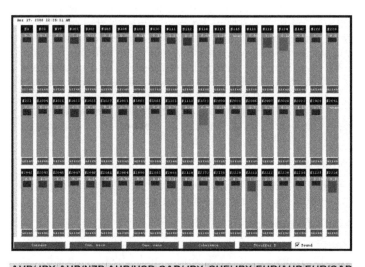

AUD/JPY	AUD/NZD	AUD/USD	CAD/JPY	CHF/JPY	EUR/AUD	EUR/CAD
86.61	1.1788	0.7324	103.02	91.60	1.6639	1.3990
86.57	1.1773	0.7321	102.98	91.56	1.6629	1.3984

EUR/CHF	EUR/CZK	EUR/DKK	EUR/GBP	EUR/HUF	EUR/JPY	EUR/NOK
1.5732	28.6730	7.4627	0.69300	268.45	144.060	7.8682
1.5728	28.6330	7.4622	0.69280	265.95	144.020	7.8632

EUR/PLN	EUR/SEK	EUR/USD	GBP/CHF	GBP/JPY	GBP/USD	NZD/USD
3.9370	9.3135	1.21835	2.27035	207.880	1.75825	0.6220
3.9270	9.3085	1.21805	2.26965	207.810	1.75785	0.6215

USD/CAD	USD/CHF	USD/DKK	USD/HKD	USD/JPY	USD/MXN	USD/NOK
1.1483	1.2914	6.1271	7.7583	118.255	11.1100	6.4602
1.1478	1.2911	6.1241	7.7578	118.225	11.0800	6.4552

USD/PLN	USD/SAR	USD/SGD	USD/THB	USD/ZAR	XAG/USD	XAU/USD
3.2327	3.7508	1.6026	37.94	6.1170	13.3200	608.30
3.2227	3.7503	1.6021	37.89	6.0870	13.2800	602.30

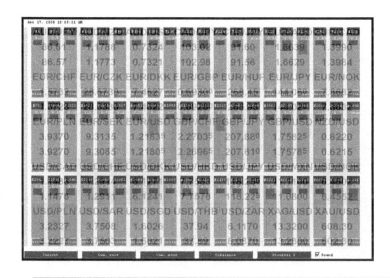

The Importance of FX Risk Management

Many are afraid of being involved with forex trading because it is 'risky'. This appears to be a very common misnomer so here we will elaborate on the potential risks of forex trading, vs. the risks of other investments and business in general, as well as outlining risk/reward and risk management policies.

First of all, currency trading especially, is not so much about gaining and losing, picking entry and exit points, but *risk management.* But herein lays the problem: if you are NOT trading forex, you are still exposed to the risks in the currency market! Even if you are not an importer or exporter, and do only domestic business, whatever your investment, it is exposed to currency risk as your investment is denominated in some dollars which are likely to appreciate or depreciate. This may not be reflected as a loss in your bank account, but you will quickly notice it in the purchasing power of your dollars, the interest rate you are getting at the bank, as well as the health of the overall economy. Therefore, it is only risky not to trade forex, because then you have a static position in certain dollars, which may be severely depreciated very quickly, at which point you can do nothing but wait for them to return to value.

Consider that the US Dollar Index was once at 120, and is now at 85. Americans who have not been making 40% to 50% per

38

year in the forex market (most likely buying Euros and selling their own US Dollars) are now exposed to high gas prices, increased commodity prices, skyrocketing real estate, and an overall shift which among other things, is destroying the middle class. It is no secret in the US that prices are increasing. However many brokers and economists are selling this to the public as profit, when in fact this is what is known as inflation. Now it costs in many places twice as much to purchase a home for your family as it did a few years ago. Wages and other income have not kept up with that price increase. This is the definition of inflation! Your dollars now can purchase less, they have less purchasing power than they did 3 or 4 years ago. So the fed says inflation is 3% a year, but really this is economic newspeak. Americans have become divided into two classes in the last few years: 1) those who are making more money than they ever dreamed of and 2) those who are struggling to make ends meet. This is transparent to previous social class structure, in other words, these 2 categories apply to the rich as well as the poor. There are for example, extremely wealthy people who are struggling to make their monthly payments because of rising financing costs, and because their investments are not doing so well. As well, there are poor people who have reaped in huge profits never seen before by investing in real estate and other high yield investments. So it is not isolated to specific demographics of people - we have become polarized economically, not politically. This was highly seen in the last Presidential election. Finally, the US economy is a benchmark for the rest of the world, for many complex factors not to be mentioned here (being the reserve currency of the world, the Petro Dollar, and being a leader in market based capitalism).

Risk Management of a forex fund

Trading forex comes down to risk management. If a forex trader takes a position in a currency, and sits on it for 3 months, while he may profit, he is exposed to the same kind of risk as if he were not trading. In other words, during that 3 month period, many things can happen to make that position open to risk. Utilizing stop losses, and actively trading, is in itself a risk management policy, rather than a strategy of knowing where the market will go. For a forex trader, the risk management side is inherently more important than guessing which direction the market will go.

It is those funds and forex traders, who are maxed to the hilt with high margins, with no stop losses, that expose their clients to the huge risks in the forex markets. Consider purchasing

100k EUR/USD at 1.2020 expecting a rise to 1.2100 (with a stop at 1.2000). If you are trading 100,000, you have taken a 100% cash position. If the EUR/USD goes as expected, you would make a profit of $800, or .8%. If it goes against you, you would lose $200, or .2%. So you are risking .2% to gain .8%. What many traders might do is take a 1,000k (1 million) position, which is 10:1 margin. This increases your P/L by 10 x - so that .2% loss is 2%, and the .8% gain is 8%. This is where risk comes into the forex market. So, it is not the forex market itself, or forex trading itself, that is risky, but rather, the risk management policy of forex dealers. Good dealers will first have a solid risk management policy, and second, develop a trading strategy.

Finally, during volatile times, or if a trader just wants to have a go at making 100 points, it is possible to take a less than 100% cash position, totally limiting the risk of loss. Using the example above, where you have 100,000 in your account, it is possible to trade 10k lots instead of 100k lots, putting you in a position of only 10% cash, or negative margin. This means the above trade loss goes from .2% to .02% - as well, your gains are also limited to .08% instead of .8%. However during certain volatile times trying to make a small profit may be better than exposing funds to potential losses.

Forex trading allows for a great degree of risk management not available in other capital markets. Margin, being able to buy or sell without limit, high liquidity (2.3 trillion traded daily), and a 24/6 market, give only the forex market to be so flexible regarding risk. In other words it is not possible to have such a sophisticated risk management policy in other markets.

- Buy OR sell (compared to stocks where you can not always go short)
- Always find a buyer or seller (the forex market is the only real liquid market in the world. It is impossible you want to trade and cannot find a buyer or seller)
- Use high margin, 200:1, or as little as you want 1:200
- Take opposite positions at the same time
- Take multiple positions (instead of selling EUR/USD, take multiple EUR positions against the crosses such as EUR/GBP, EUR/CHF, as a hedge against your first EUR/USD position)

The above factors are the real opportunities in the forex market, not the potential to make 100% that exist in other markets such as the stock market.

How stop-losses work

Whenever you take a forex position, you always have the ability to enter a stop-loss order. This means no matter what happens, if the position goes against you, you will exit at the pre defined stop loss order. If for example you purchase 100k of EUR/USD at 1.2050 expecting the EUR/USD to rise in value, and your stop is placed at 1.2020, you are guaranteed to be filled at your price, even if the EUR/USD drops to 1.1700. Using stop losses can be a great addition to a risk management policy.

Market conditions

There are times in the forex market where the market is extremely volatile, such as when the Fed makes an interest rate announcement, or during the first few hours of major market openings, such as 9:00 am - 11:00 am New York Time.

Risk Profile

Every trader or investor in the forex market should have a solid risk profile. Your risk capital will determine the risk-profile of your account. For example, if you have 10,000 to invest, you can say that you are willing to risk 1,000 of that capital with the potential to gain another 10,000. This can be easily implemented by a fund manager, so your losses can be limited to 10% or 5% of invested capital. It is not impossible, but would be very reckless, for someone to lose 100% or even 50% of invested capital in less than a year. That means they are using high margins and purchasing more than the account's risk profile can handle. This is not only unprofessional, it is dangerous and bad for the client and the industry. Clients may have pre-arranged agreements with their forex dealer what is the risk profile of their capital. It may be that you are willing to take high-risks, but it should all be discussed and agreed upon before your account is traded.

Risks of not trading

Business itself carries a high degree of risk. Clients may not come to your shop. Payments may not go through. Factories have malfunctions. For those who claim forex trading is risky, as explained above it can be (with a reckless dealer). But consider the risks of not trading. Consider a scenario where the EU dissolves, and the Euro is no more. Every investor who is in the Euro (such as the common European and foreign investors alike) would have huge, nearly incalculable losses. Americans are subject to the same risk. With a seemingly unstable political environment, a current account deficit and government deficit spiraling out of control, it is quite possible to see the US dollar lose 80% of its value in a very short time frame.

In conclusion, there is an inherit risk in forex which exists in any capital market, but the risk is not in the market itself, but rather, in the risk management policy of the forex dealer, and in the structure of how the funds are traded. Before investing in the forex market discuss your risk profile with your funds manager, to make sure this is right for you, or if it can be adjusted to fit your risk profile.

The above is meant to explain the risks of forex trading in more detail, it does not in any way suggest forex trading is risk - free. Also it is not the recommendation that anyone puts more money into forex trading than they can afford to lose. This gives dealers the flexibility to relax and trade as they want (vs. trying to make 1% per week or a certain performance benchmark). A typical investment in the forex market may comprise 10% to 20% of an investor's portfolio.

Unintended consequence

The **Law of Unintended Consequences** holds that almost all human actions have at least one unintended consequence. In other words, each cause has more than one effect, including *unforeseen effects*. The idea dates to the Scottish Enlightenment, which influenced people such as Thomas Jefferson. [iv]

Chapter 3: Technical Analysis

Do they mean anything?

Technical analysis has long been a widely used technique in determining market trends. Analysts proficient in their trade, see expressive animated objects in charts. After staring at charts for 20 years – you would see things too. Try laying down in the ground and looking at the clouds for over an hour. Do you have the patience? You will see shapes and faces of friends.

However there are patterns in the markets and anyone who says otherwise needs to have their head examined. Definitely, the markets are random. But in the randomness there are short term patters. Technical analysis is NOT a method to predict the market. However, it can act as a stable guideline to indicate price action in the short term.

Levels

One very important part of FX technicals are natural support and resistance. Unlike equity markets which do not have real support (meaning a panic could cause an 80% drop in a matter of minutes) FX markets are backed by central banks – the wealthiest organizations on the planet. Actually, central banks have the ability to print money so it is difficult to describe them in terms of 'wealth' – but the point here is they have deep pockets. If the USD started crashing, it could easily be supported by the Fed, ECB, or any combination of minor banks. Political or economic factors may determine real money demand for supporting the dollar at certain levels.

Chart Freaks

Another significant thing about FX technicals is that those who have a degree of influence on large FX trades, like to see nice looking charts. They are the kind of people who have a meticulously trimmed mustache, and a spike on the chart just wouldn't be tidy. In the land of Mary Poppins traders have a unique view that charts should look a certain way. Driving the dollar down 15 pips may seem totally insignificant in the short term, but it creates a certain technical picture on the hourlies. Don't forget this is on the mind of dealers who have an influence on large FX positions.

Price Protection

Traders with positions in other markets which are affected by spot FX, may use the interbank market to protect their positions in other markets – most typically FX options. For example if there are a significant options expiring if the USD/JPY reaches below 20 – large money may sell USD/JPY in an attempt to drive down the cross putting their options positions in the money. Their spot FX positions may lose, even heavily, but it's a small insurance against their options.

How to identify a real move vs. technical trend

Technicals are most significant when the market is quiet, or during periods of consolidation.   When in a trading range, price channels start to form. An example of when technicals DO NOT apply is during a major data release, Fed Decision, or major news event. If there is a panic in the market, technicals may only act as points of support and resistance and should NOT be relied on for trading.

Tolerance

Have a degree of tolerance to support and resistance levels, price channels, and trend lines, which is appropriate for the time frame you are analyzing. The larger the time frame, the larger the tolerance should be. 5 pips can throw you off, and you think it's a breakout, but it's just a small price spike. A breakout should be well-defined and sustained.

Time Frames

Real pros trade dailies. Trading anything other than dailies, is scalping, pretty much. In the dailies you can see long term trends that develop, and you can make 1,000 pips per trade on the dailies.

Counter trending - Go against the trend

"Remember, the trend is your friend", they say. There are many strategies that involve identifying a trend – but very few, if any – that go against the trend. Why? If that were the case, the market would be in a consistent state of up or down (single direction). Clearly, that is not the case, the market is subject to whipsaws at the whim of news events or other unexpected phenomena.   Counter trending is a more successful strategy for trading.   Instead of identifying a trend, identify when a trend is over.

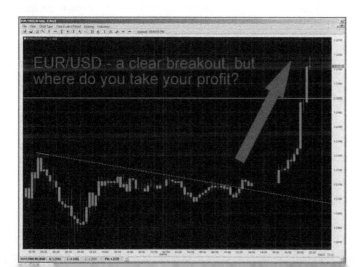

Fibonacci

One very important part of FX technicals are natural support and resistance. Unlike equity markets which do not have real support (meaning a panic could cause an 80% drop in a matter of minutes) FX markets are backed by central banks – the wealthiest organizations on the planet. Actually, central banks have the ability to print money so it is difficult to describe them in terms of 'wealth' – but the point here is they have deep pockets. If the USD started crashing, it could easily be supported by the Fed, ECB, or any combination of minor banks. Political or economic factors may determine real money demand for supporting the dollar at certain levels.

Mathematical Advantage

If you trade a Fibonacci retracement, and correctly identify a top or bottom, you can calculate different Fibonacci levels that it should retrace to. However, if you trade a break, where do you take your profit? There is no way to extrapolate a breakout to determine where the move will stop.

Less volatile, less risk

Usually retracements are more organized, orderly trade, than a frantic buy or sell. A retracement is an after-the-fact, traders who changed their mind or are taking their profit, and more orderly, than knee-jerk reactions to data or news events. There is much less risk trading a retracement, than trading a breakout.

Mathematics

Many market participants in FX market do not have basic math skills. This goes for traders and clients. Here we will outline a few notable FX mathematical examples.

Account Returns Math

Clients always want to see huge returns with no risk. 26% doesn't excite them but 260% does. All you have to do, is turn on the leverage faucet. But when any drawdown happens, greed becomes fear and results in complaints and frustration.

See the below charts. Assuming you NET 50% returns per month, after fees, in 2 years, $1,000 becomes 11m and respectively, 10,000 becomes 100 million. There have been no reported cases of this ever happening. Even Soros who is known as a famous currency trader, has never made returns like this.

Month	Capital	Month	Capital
1	$10,000.00	1	$1,000.00
2	$15,000.00	2	$1,500.00
3	$22,500.00	3	$2,250.00
4	$33,750.00	4	$3,375.00
5	$50,625.00	5	$5,062.50
6	$75,937.50	6	$7,593.75
7	$113,906.25	7	$11,390.63
8	$170,859.38	8	$17,085.94
9	$256,289.06	9	$25,628.91
10	$384,433.59	10	$38,443.36
11	$576,650.39	11	$57,665.04
12	$864,975.59	12	$86,497.56
13	$1,297,463.38	13	$129,746.34
14	$1,946,195.07	14	$194,619.51
15	$2,919,292.60	15	$291,929.26
16	$4,378,938.90	16	$437,893.89
17	$6,568,408.36	17	$656,840.84
18	$9,852,612.53	18	$985,261.25
19	$14,778,918.80	19	$1,477,891.88
20	$22,168,378.20	20	$2,216,837.82
21	$33,252,567.30	21	$3,325,256.73
22	$49,878,850.95	22	$4,987,885.10
23	$74,818,276.43	23	$7,481,827.64
24	$112,227,414.64	24	$11,222,741.46

The 100% fallacy

A 100% return means your account doubles. If you start with 1,000 and make 1,000 that is considered to be a 100% return. Some claim to be able to make 100% consistently, when the math clearly shows how this is impossible.

If you start with only $1,000 in your trading account, and double every month:

•   In 1 year, you will have $64,000 or a 6,400 % return (64x your investment)

•   In 2 years, you will have $262 million

•   In 3 years, you will have $1 trillion

•   Finally, after 4 years, you would have $4 quadrillion, more money than exists in the entire world!

Why mention this? Keep this in mind when looking at returns. 25% per year doesn't look so bad, when looking at this chart.

Also, consider the dynamics of trading large funds. The above chart displays what would happen if you start with $1,000 – what if you

$	1,000.00
$	2,000.00
$	4,000.00
$	8,000.00
$	16,000.00
$	32,000.00
$	**64,000.00**
$	128,000.00
$	256,000.00
$	512,000.00
$	1,024,000.00
$	2,048,000.00
$	4,096,000.00
$	8,192,000.00
$	16,384,000.00
$	32,768,000.00
$	65,536,000.00
$	131,072,000.00
$	**262,144,000.00**
$	524,288,000.00
$	1,048,576,000.00
$	2,097,152,000.00
$	4,194,304,000.00
$	8,388,608,000.00
$	16,777,216,000.00
$	33,554,432,000.00
$	67,108,864,000.00
$	134,217,728,000.00
$	268,435,456,000.00
$	536,870,912,000.00
$	**1,073,741,824,000.00**
$	2,147,483,648,000.00
$	4,294,967,296,000.00
$	8,589,934,592,000.00
$	17,179,869,184,000.00
$	34,359,738,368,000.00
$	68,719,476,736,000.00
$	137,438,953,472,000.00
$	274,877,906,944,000.00
$	549,755,813,888,000.00
$	1,099,511,627,776,000.00
$	2,199,023,255,552,000.00
$	**4,398,046,511,104,000.00**

start with $1,000,000? Would those returns even be possible?

Pip values are calculated in base currency

EUR/USD has a pip value of 1 USD because USD is the currency you are exchanging for 1 euro. Your P/L is floating in USD because when you click, you are taking 1 virtual Euro and exchanging it for 'x' amount of USD – the number of USD you get in return changes – what is fixed is the 1 Euro it cost you upon purchasing. Therefore your pips are calculated in USD. It's simple for x/USD crosses to be calculated, especially if you have a USD based account. 10 pips = 10 USD. 150 pips = 150 USD; simple. But when you start trading EUR/GBP and GBP/JPY it gets complex – or does it?

Chapter 4: Strategies

FX Strategy

Develop winning strategies

A strategy is a set of rules which you will follow – manually or automatically it adds up to the same definition. The strategy is how you will trade your FX account. A strategy is the opposite of a bet. Even an educated bet is gambling. It is of course possible to gamble using FX due to the fact that you can click and have a profit or loss – but that is a sure way to lose in the long term.

Run multiple strategies

One strategy never works. It may work some of the time, or even MOST of the time, but never ALL the time. If there was a strategy that worked all the time, none of us would be trading, we would be investing in that strategy.

Also, what gives electronic markets such volatility is the disagreement of positions (traders having opposite strategies), i.e. I want to buy and you want to sell.

How can you do this, when you have 1 account? Develop a strategy for each pair – a EUR/USD strategy, a EUR/CHF strategy, and a GBP/JPY strategy, each with conflicting rules. Just by nature of this approach, it is statistically less probable that you will lose money. Randomly, as long as you chose uncorrelated strategies, you should be at least net flat, even if you don't know what you're doing.

That doesn't mean the strategies should be opposite it means they should be uncorrelated, for example the EUR/USD strategy only trades the news, whereas the EUR/GBP strategy trades Bollinger Bands and RSI on the hourly chart.

Refco EUR Sunday

Before the demise of Refco, there was a small pattern of EUR/USD going up every Sunday before the rest of the FX markets came in. Sometimes it was 10 pips, sometimes 50. Never 100. Sometimes it would stay up for an hour, sometimes 5 minutes, but it ALWAYS went back to the open before 6pm NY time, when other markets were coming into the market. The reason this happened is irrelevant, the significant point is it happened every Sunday for 3 months!

Small patterns can determine simple strategies.

Fibonacci Money Management Strategy

Money management can be more important than price action.

48

For the most obvious example, being right 10 pips on 1 lot is peanuts but on 1000 lots is great. So it's not about pips, it's about position size. During a big move, you don't know where the EUR/USD will end up – where will it stop?

Assume in this example you are trading 100,000 USD, but in 10,000 increments. You start by shorting – pick any level you think may be the top. As it goes up, you continue shorting using fibo levels to determine your size. 1, 2, 3, 5, 8, .. and so on. The amount in price the euro will need to retrace, in order for your position to be profitable, is constantly decreasing, as your size increases. But it is increasing as the price is going up, thus creating a higher probability every time that the currency will retrace. If you have 1:1 odds for your 1 lot, you have 2:1 on your 2 lot, and so on.

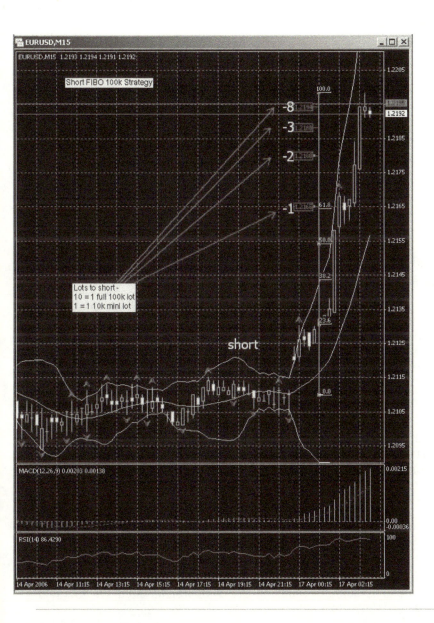

How to be a profitable trader

Everyone has a different trading style. There is no perfect formula for trading. If there were, it could be codified and run automatically. There still is a human element in trading, which only a human trader can feel.

3 trading rules:

- The only thing you can do to determine your trading style, is trade.
- The only way to learn how to trade (or trade well) is to trade.
- The only real tips and tools for trading can be obtained, by trading.

Keep this in mind when looking through books and other guides to trading. They are all different trader's approaches, and the truth, for you, lies somewhere in between.

Most importantly:

- Have confidence in your abilities and ideas
- Don't be discouraged if your ideas don't work out
- Always be on the lookout for other ideas
- Once you are in a trade, don't second guess yourself. **Stick to your plan!**

Make a trading plan.

A trading plan, much like a business plan, outlines your strategy technically and from a money management perspective. A good plan can have a poor outcome, and conversely, a poorly designed plan can have a positive (profitable) outcome. Making a good trading plan and sticking to it are key to unlocking the mental discipline necessary to be a good trader.

Don't have an ego

There are so many tools a trader can use in his strategy arsenal; there is no reason not to use them. No one can predict the markets, no matter how smart you are. Use the tools available to you. Use signals services, market analysis, trading strategies, which have already been tested. There have been billions of dollars poured into strategy development in the forex business, and some of the smartest people in the world have spent years developing solid trading strategies. Who are you to compete? Many of them offer signal services or technical analysis services either for a fee or for free.

Don't let your ego get in the way of these tools and techniques. Let the systems and computers do the work for you! What a real trader is doing is watching the computer assisted systems and making sure they don't have bugs.

FX Day Trading 101 - 5 Techniques

There are five common basic strategies by which day traders attempt to make a profit: Trend following, playing news events, range trading, scalping, and technical trading.

Trend following - Trend following, a strategy used in all trading time frames, assumes that currencies which have been rising steadily will continue to rise, and vice versa. The trend follower buys a currency which has been rising, or short-sells a falling currency, in the expectation that the trend will continue.

Playing News - Playing news is primarily the realm of the day trader. The basic strategy is to buy a currency which has just announced good news, or short-sell on bad news. Such events provide enormous volatility in a currency and therefore the greatest chance for quick profits (or losses).

Range Trading - A range trader watches a currency that has been rising off a support price and falling off a resistance price. That is, every time the currency hits a high, it falls back to the low, and vice versa. Such a stock is said to be "trading in a range". The range trader therefore buys the currency at or near the low price, and sells (and possibly short sells) at the high. Scalping - Scalping originally referred to spread trading. Today it has come to mean any extremely quick trade for a small profit.

Technical Analysis - What Is Technical Analysis? Technical analysis is a method of evaluating the markets value by analyzing statistics generated by market activity, past prices and volume. Technical analysts do not attempt to measure a vehicle's intrinsic value; instead they look at charts for patterns and indicators that will determine future performance. Technical analysis has become increasingly popular over the past several years, as more and more people believe that the historical performance is a strong indication of future performance. The use of past performance should come as no surprise. People using fundamental analysis have always looked at the past performance of companies by comparing fiscal data from previous quarters and years to determine future growth. The difference lies in the technical analyst's belief that securities move according to very predictable trends and patterns. These trends continue until something happens to change the trend, and until this change occurs, price levels are predictable.

Scalping – Scalping is a day-trader's arb, seeing an opportunity to make a quick 5 – 30 pips and taking a huge position. The thinking is that if you can scalp 10 pips, safely, 10 times a day, it's the same as being right on a larger 100 pip move. Scalpers are discouraged in FX, especially on accounts with dealers. Some 'sniper' scalpers can actually try and exploit small price moves initiated by dealers, essentially 'trading against the dealers'. Any scalping in FX is low-brow and considered less than ethical – and for good reason. In this case you are just exploiting inefficiencies in price action, not actually doing anything useful for the markets.

Triangulation

There are many arb strategies commonly known in the banking FX trading community which date back to the roots of FX market making. Triangular arb, for example, exploits the difference between 3 crosses. For example a move in EUR/USD implies a move in EUR/CHF and USD/CHF but those other 2 crosses need to be sold and reflect the move in EUR/USD. Markets are so liquid today that these arb opportunities are very rare, and your trades may anyhow be rejected if you find one. However, you can play 3 currencies against each other which can give you net positions in the currency you really want to play. Some platforms will display net positions in USD, JPY, etc.

Quiet market scalping in a channel

This is a common strategy, and like it or not, there is no other way to trade if the market is dead.

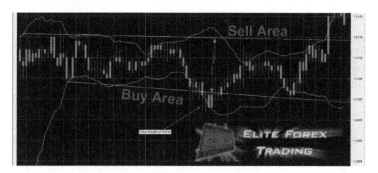

During this above time period of 2 days, it would have been possible to clear the 15 pip difference 8 times, for a total of 120 pips. Doesn't sound like much, but this is the chance to increase the leverage. In this case, you can feel comfortable taking a 10 x position, multiplying your potential to 1,200 pips, on 1 cross. Of course that is your theoretical maximum. Realistically, you shouldn't START with 10x lots, start with 2x or 3x, then, only as you have a profit, increase your trade size every time you reverse. Have a % stop large enough to make it through the fake breakout on the bottom, and to get taken near the top which is a real breakout. With all the stops this strategy could net 1,000 or 800 pips using the chart shown, in 2 days.

This could be seen as a form of scalping, although it also falls into the category of range trading.

Swing Trading

See below swing trading report with EUR/USD. EUR got sold off huge today, and we got a buy signal for potential retracement. It became an interesting trade as the 5minute chart quickly turned into a nicely bound range of tops and bottoms.

Total profit: 8% in 8 hours

Leverage used: 10:1 up to 20:1

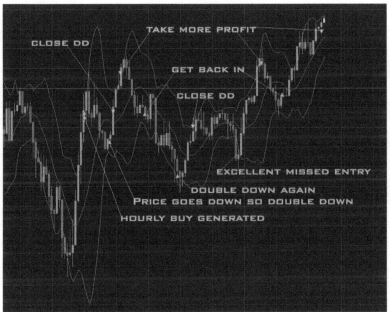

Trades were 100% positive, or, there were no losing trades.

This may seem ridiculous, but now look how insignificant these trades look on the hourly chart:

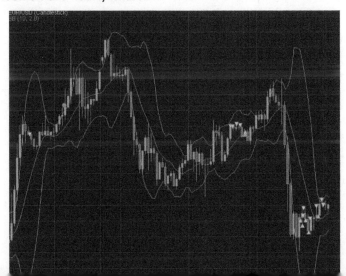

On the above hourly they look like a bunch of junk trades, yet they produced 8% with little or no risk (if you know what you are doing). Now, the significance of this swing trading strategy is that it came after such a large downmove in the EUR/USD. The fundamentals as to WHY the EUR/USD moved down so quickly are irrelevant, the relevant point is that we feel confident that it has made its move, and will retrace, but not too quickly. The market was in a state of shock, and from another hourly perspective, it looks quite dead:

Now looking at the above chart, all this activity we're talking about

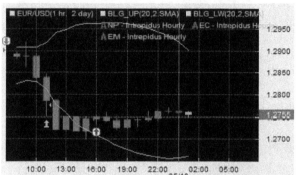

was generated due to this buy signal. The signal turned out to be a dud, but it was turned into some real action on the 5 minute. The entire time, our bias was towards the upside due to the hourly signal, and knowing the large move down needed to retrace a little by profit takers. So on the 5 minute our strategy was to load up when nearing the bottom Bollinger band.

Automatic Strategies

There are many platforms and ways to code and test any strategy quickly using script languages such as MetaQuotes, Intelliscript, or EasyLanguage. Each was designed with traders in mind that you don't have to be a programmer to code a successful strategy. While this is not exactly easy, still, you can find a programmer on the Internet who may code your strategy for $100 or $200.

Once you have this, you can do valid backtesting of your strategy to see how it would have worked in many market conditions. This is a very powerful tool, as it will calculate exact points rather than a trader manually backtesting.

Auto-trading Strategies

The ultimate level of automation in FX is a strategy that trades itself, totally. In some cases, traders influence the style of trading implemented by the strategy, lot sizes, and other factors. But the strategy trades on its own without any human intervention. Think of the software equivalent of a Macro – it's not fully blown software, it's a script that has predefined criteria such as:

```
IF CrossDown(EMA(Close,5) , EMA(Close,10)) THEN
    AddSellEntry
ENDIF
```

--OR--

```
IF RSI > 70 THEN
AddSellEntry
```

These represent simple strategies to display how logical arguments are codified connected to the markets. With hundreds of functions, hundreds of indicators, and many time frames, strategies can quickly become complex. Software allows you to take this codified strategy and backtest it with varying degrees of accuracy, to see if your strategy works.

Automation flaws

The dark side of automation lies in its being – it is automated. There is no human control, no common sense. Markets however are ultimately controlled by emotional, irrational humans. When the greater majority of FX trading is done automatically, this may change. But for the time being, the majority of FX volume is by human or human strategy. Keep in mind this does not mean execution automation, a technical function – it is being referred to is decision automation, or strategy automation.

The largest problem of making automated strategies is they are never perfect. Any strategy, given enough time, will fail. The only strategy that can continuously, consistently succeed is one that is constantly changing. As yet, a system like this does not exist.

FX Signals & Alerts

The ultimate question of the relevance of the signals and alerts is, if the alerts are optimized, why not just auto trade them – isn't that the ultimate? Why manually trade when signals clearly work.

The answer to that is simple and complex at the same time. Also there are many personal and professional reasons why a good FX trader will use signals even in his manual / discretionary trading.

BIAS –RSI is not going to pinpoint exact entry levels. However, overbought and oversold RSI levels do indicate a bias. That's why these tools are called indicators and not alerts or strategies, they

INDICATE price action, not dictate. When we have a pricing model which will forecast price movement 10 bars out we will not call it an indicator it will be called a dictator.

MANUAL OVERRIDE – Many do not fully trust automated systems. And they do have bugs – even the most robust systems are prone to human error, power outages, etc. Many systems are automatically generated by black box systems while trades are manually entered by humans.

NOT ENOUGH REASON TO CODIFY – Some systematic systems are so simple it wouldn't be worth the complication and expense to codify them.

COMMON SENSE – It doesn't take a genius to realize that if there is a bomb in London the Pound will go down. But news cannot be quantified at an accurate level. Traders still need to rely on their instinct and experience even when dealing with fully automated systems.

The Auto-trading Art

After watching automated systems such as Meta Trader Expert Advisors trade, traders may discover patters in the strategy that cannot be coded. However, they can be shut down and restarted for a decent profit (or missing a loss). Strategies always work in certain time frames, i.e. In a week strategy A may have 80% winners but in week 2 it only has 20% winners. This can be due to a number of unquantifiable events, but basically a trader can kill or fill strategies themselves much like trades. A trader must decide if the signal for EUR/USD is correct before pulling the trigger, and in the same light can decide if Intrepidus strategy has a handle on this market.

Auto-trading Analytics – what to look for

Part of being a good trader is knowing what to look for. Backtesting may not guarantee future results, but it gives you an entire picture of how a strategy behaves. If you really want to analyze a strategy properly, you can go date by date and trade by trade, seeing what news was driving the markets that day. But just glancing at backtesting reports know what to look for. Take a look at this Meta Trader report:

The most important piece of info, in the case of MT reports, is 'Modeling Quality'. Many MT brokers don't provide proper tick data to do backtesting and therefore the backtests always make money and always are totally wrong. See here the modeling quality is 89.73% - acceptably high (The higher the %, the better). Now this above backtest produced these 'live' results:

There is a list of trades you can see as attachments at the end of this book; the above is a graphic representation. There really are only a few important things to notice:

• drawdowns (how much the trade is negative before being positive)

• drawdowns per trade and drawdowns for the entire account (you see how the account dips down before becoming positive)

• Winners vs. losers ratio (you see Profit trades % of total is 77%. If that was 20% you should worry)

All of these bits and pieces add up to a behavior of a strategy. A good auto trading portfolio should have a balanced mix of uncorrelated strategies. There are different ways to calculate 'un-correlation' but suffice to look for strategies that profit during different kinds of market conditions with different crosses.

Auto-trading Platforms

The most common auto-trading platforms offer traders 'script languages' to describe their strategy in code. The leader of this has been Tradestation Securities, although they have been slow to adopt Forex and subsequently have a lot of competition.

Tradestation

TradeStation is charting software and system design all rolled into the one platform. It has fast become one of the most highly-acclaimed trading platforms for active traders because it offers two key capabilities:

1. Develop and back-test trading strategies
TradeStation offers you a risk-free method designed to help you pinpoint trading strategies that have worked year after year based on historical data. Its premiere EasyLanguage® technology lets you communicate virtually any custom trading idea imaginable (when you'd like to buy, and when you'd like to sell) to your computer.

Then, with just a click of your mouse, it back-tests your idea on up to 20 years of actual, intra-day market data and shows you the simulated results. All the trades you would have placed, your simulated net profit or loss, and much more-before you risk one cent of real trading capital.

2. **Automated Trading**

TradeStation is also designed to help you identify market opportunities and execute your trades more efficiently than you could ever do manually. It actually monitors the markets for you-tick-by-tick, in real-time-and seeks market opportunities based on your strategies.

The instant an opportunity arises based on your custom buy or sell rules, it's designed to automatically generate your entry and exit orders and send them to the marketplace-within fractions of a second of the market move.

With TradeStation's powerful EasyLanguage, you'll be able to describe and test your own custom strategies.

EasyLanguage is the custom programming language used by TradeStation. As with any programming language, it can take time to

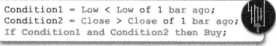

```
Condition1 = Low < Low of 1 bar ago;
Condition2 = Close > Close of 1 bar ago;
If Condition1 and Condition2 then Buy;
```

About EasyLanguage

Since its introduction just over a decade ago, EasyLanguage has become an industry standard used by professional traders to test trading strategies.

become familiar with the syntax requirements and structure in order to program complex trading system strategies.

TradeStation comes with a comprehensive EasyLanguage reference which provides information on all aspects of the programming language. Due to the popularity of TradeStation as a charting, trading platform, you will find that many EasyLanguage examples can be found on the internet.

Meta Trader

MetaTrader 4, is an online trading complex designed to provide broker services to customers at Forex, Futures and CFD markets. This is a whole-cycle complex, which means that you won't need any more software to organize your broker services, if using MetaTrader 4.

MetaTrader 4 Client Terminal has a user friendly front-end trading interface. Provides technical analysis, charting and expert advisors to develop own trading strategies.[v]

Elite FX eGraph

Our Solution: Signals in charts

There are many signal providers on the internet. Which one is the best? How will I know it will work over time? So many providers, too few time to evaluate them.

Elite E Services has a solution: An integrated package that combines a professional forex charting package, with signal plug-ins. That means you can plug-in the strategy that you want. Choose from a list of strategies, or make your own. Instead of switching signal providers every month, have your own signals software.

We don't think any strategy or signal system can profit consistently, in the long run. Our solution is to constantly develop NEW Strategies, as well as optimizing old ones. We have seen the rise and fall of many providers over the years, now we will try to solve the unsolvable: To provide a family of uncorrelated profitable strategies constantly being optimized and tested.

Elite FX eGraph : The future of FX Signals and Charting

Software features

FX Email yourself signals, for auto-trading or for SMS alerts

FX Customize how YOU WANT to use the signals on specific charts and specific time frames

FX Do your own backtesting, to see how various systems are working with various market conditions

FX Use MULTIPLE strategies at the same time (for example you can have an AUD/NZD strategy running in conjunction with a EUR/USD strategy, they are uncorrelated).

FX See how different versions of the same strategy work

FX Customize the alerts to make sounds, getting your attention.

EES can also code your custom strategy in this platform. Do you want to receive alerts based on your own strategy? With this platform, we can code a simple strategy for you for only $100 USD. You will get the code, backtests, optimizations, and different strategies.

FX Features of Elite FX eGraph:

FX Group Setting saving feature

FX Export/Download data

FX Local time zones

FX Choose from 2 data feed providers

FX Customizable Fibonacci Retracements

FX Easy one-click printing

FX Indicator Combination; e.g. Apply Bollinger Bands on RSI

FX Complete suite of Technical Indicators

FX Over 5-dozen Time Scale/Periods, including tick & historical

FX Save your own user settings

FX Available in Chinese, Japanese, and Polish

FX Streaming quotes

FX Includes access to both Online and Desktop services!

FX Desktop only $100/month - datafeed is included!

Elite FX eGraph is a white label of FX Trek Intellicharts. If you have Intellicharts, our systems will work with your platform. With Elite FX eGraph, however, you get our signals, systems, plugins, groupfiles, and access to eesFX.com with additional tools and plugins.[vi]

Smaller Apps

There are smaller apps less developed such as TradeItself. While not exactly a platform, TradeItself will take email signals you send to it and automatically 'press' buttons in your FXCM software.

TradeItself 2006 is software which collects and converts emails to trades for FXCM. The software provides extensive configuration capabilities for reading trading instructions from emails. TradeItself 2006 bridges the gap between your FOREX email signals and your FXCM account.
No third party email client required

- Trade multiple FXCM logins and accounts
- Over 20 trading instructions available
- Price, stop loss, limit, trading instructions and currencies can be read from email
- Place market and entry orders
- FXCM trading station not required to be running
- Limit and stop loss can be dynamically offset from entry price

API Environments

The highest level of auto-trading involves an API – Application Program Interface. The API is the pure data-feed into the FX brokerage, without software. Clients on the other side then develop either software or a 'black box' – namely, a system that analyzes market data and executes trades without anyone knowing what it's doing. Below is explanation from Oanda:

The API provides the ability to submit trade requests, set and modify stop-loss/take-profit/entry orders, obtain historical transactions and both current and historical FXTrade market rates and candlesticks.

A library is dynamically linked to the customer systems, and implements the FXTrade protocol, communicating directly with OANDA's FXTrade servers over secure and authenticated Internet sessions. It does not require that the FXTrade User Interface be running at the same time, but the customer may use the Interface to monitor in real time any actions taken by the customer systems using the API.

Features

- Simple to understand; easy to work with
- Secure, authenticated sessions over fully encrypted communication channels
- Available in both Java and C++
- Unlimited risk-free testing on FXGame systems

Who would benefit from using the API?

The OANDA FXTrade system offers a long list of benefits to foreign exchange traders, such as 7/24 availability, the tightest spreads in Forex, immediate execution with full transparency, flexible deal sizes, continuous interest and multi-currency accounts.

Each of these is now available to customers who wish to build automated Forex systems, including:

- Forex Brokers, Hedge Funds and Money Managers seeking to hedge exposure
- Treasuries with frequent Forex dealings that wish to integrate FX trading into their treasury systems
- Brokers who wish to hedge the exchange rate exposure of their equity positions
- Corporations requiring frequent, real-time Forex hedging capabilities
- Customers who wish to develop their own, customized user interface to OANDA's FXTrade system
- Retail customers developing proprietary trading models

vii

How to build a working forex strategy

This guide was written with MQL in mind but could work for any scripting language. The idea of the scripting language should not be overcomplicated – the language serves as a set of commands which will tell your strategy how to behave.

Components of a working strategy:

1. Filters – You should have to meet several global criteria before looking for signals. Filters could be time of day, volatility, or indicator based. Each strategy should have several filters which should be adjustable by the user. Too many filters will produce no trades.

2. Inputs – When coding, make use of inputs as much as possible. Instead of 'hard coding' a value into a strategy, declare it as a global variable or global input which can be changed later without actually changing the code.

3. Fungible – Strategy should port well to other time frames and crosses. Once you have the template you can make specific strategies for specific circumstances such as the EUR/JPY version or the EUR/USD 5 minute.

4. Money Management – Strategy should have solid money management which is outside the realm of the actual signal / strategy. The money management module of the strategy is almost a strategy by itself. If you have the correct signal to buy, how many lots do you buy? This question is more important than what price to buy.

Choose your set of indicators and stick to finding patterns within those indicators. We prefer Bollinger Bands because they are based on standard deviations. One could literally make hundreds of strategies just based on Bollinger Bands.

Look at the charts and try to determine patterns. When making the strategy attempt to make it such that you can slightly adjust the pattern rule for testing – the first pattern you program will not likely be a profitable one.

Inputs can be optimized, so if you want to find the best setting amoung a group it is best to program 'x'.

The order in which commands are executed can influence the results of the strategy so be careful to order syntax commands in the logical order you want. Programming a trading strategy is unlike programming a software application, because the syntax can compile correctly and there can be an unoptimized order of instructions. There are many ways to code the same strategy, each which may result in varying results.

Most strategies are rule based on bars. A bar is the time value based on the chart that is displayed. For example on the below 30 minute chart each bar represents 30 minutes.

Take the example of the 30 Minute EUR/USD Chart:

Charts that are statistically important for strategy idea generation:

15 minute, 30 minute, 1 hour, 4 hour, 1 day.

The 5 minute time frame is so small many events mathematically displayed on the 5 minute may be aberrations and not true trading signals.

How can we make a rule to generate a buy signal?

If the previous 3 bars are below the Bollinger band, then sell.

Each entry signal should be integrated with the money management module. So now we have a sell signal – which is sent to the MM module, which will tell us (based on account value, margin requirements, and other settings) what SIZE of a position to trade.

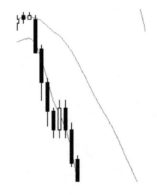

Chapter 5: FX Life & Experience

You cannot trade your way to freedom

It is impossible to use FX as a method of gaining riches, getting out of a job you hate or other bad situation, or using forex market to get famous. This is the path toward catastrophe.

Unfortunately, due to the leverage and some reported high performance of notable FX funds, the FX trading community has garnered a reputation in the internet community and others as being a way you can trade and get rich. This idea is proliferated by a low-class group of so called 'affiliate' marketers who dwell on the greed and hopes of poor souls who are searching subconsciously for a financial break.

This is frowned upon by any ethical trader. They say in a crooked environment, crooks are the most honest people. In financial services, most do not have the luxury of existing in the grey area, because of the potential liability. However those promoting forex in this manner are not in financial services industry, in fact they are not in any professional industry at all. There is no law to stop them from writing anything they choose on their website, as the internet is a free say anything you like domain. That by itself is harmless, but they are creating an aura of credibility by linking to each other as references, and creating a campaign of believers who further consolidate their position, and it is unfortunate because many do fall victim to their schemes. The sad story is that financial professionals would not attract the kind of attention received by these marketers.

Live Debt Free

At any level of FX business, whether you are a trader or broker, you should be cash, and debt free. You can't trade for your next bill, trade for a living, or trade to pay off a bill. This is a sure fire way to lose all your funds.

Trading Zen

Trading is like meditating. Each trader should have the right set of circumstances, the right mind frame, the right everything. The slightest interruption, distraction, can ruin your path to pips. It could be irrelevant, a delivery guy, a dog, a screaming kid. A real dealing room should be modeled after Buddhist monasteries, not hectic wall street offices. It is not to criticize hectic offices, but this is not for trading – it's for sales. In fact many successful big name traders live in very remote areas on farms, trading with their computer equipment and satellite Internet connections.

Trading is Blue Collar

You wake up early, you see an opportunity, and you click a few buttons, and go to lunch. There is nothing elite, intellectual, or otherwise sophisticated in FX trading.

In some ways, being an FX trader is really hard work – like digging a ditch. You have your tools, you have your clients who by the way only pay per performance, and you're only as good as your last trade. To top it off, you are constantly on the verge of being sued, whether it is by some crackpot webmaster or angry client that just lost his divorce case.

Waking up at 6am and working until 9pm or later, losing your nerves and being on the verge of liability if you are trading for clients – what can be better than that (other than a stick in the eye)?

Who is an FX trader?

I suppose there is a target audience for these statements, I mean if you are working at a bank this is totally different. We are however trying to describe an entire spectrum of new FX traders. Traders can trade from anywhere, be anyone. Also we are not discriminating against the trading establishment, because they are the primary mover behind many of these changes.

Traders do have a different approach to the markets, and lifestyle is the best way to describe this approach. Trading 9-5 for example may not be feasible. Your lifestyle should fit your trading style.

Who is FX?

Someone who works for a bank? Someone who stares at cross rates for 10 hours a day? The programmers who make the software behind the traders? The banks? "they're not FX" ..they say.

Rural self-sufficiency

One ideal setup is to be on a farm or other rural property, a totally independent self-sufficient compound which does not require monthly payment, maintenance, hassle, or time. If you can have that, it will greatly influence your ability to see the markets. You need to create an FX monastery from which you will be able to forecast the FX future. That may sound really bizarre, but it's really a hyperbole. It doesn't have to be rural, it may be industrial, but several criteria need to be satisfied:

• Debt free (you have no monthly payments)

• Quiet (you can hear animals but not screaming humans)

• Fast Internet (satellite has a delay which is unacceptable with FX)

• Spacious (should not be cramped, have enough room for you

to setup how you want)

- Private FX Dealing room (away from your living space, you should have a room which is 'just FX')

If you think this idea is far-fetched, why did Saxo Bank build such a facility? In fact they have totally shut down their downtown office, and now operate from a 'bucolic trading facility' 20 minutes out of town. It's equipped with servers, a cafe, and health spa.

FOREX IS ECO-FRIELDLY

Investing in the currency market is done electronically and requires no paperwork. Investing in currency does not promote the harming of any living creatures. No burning of fossil fuels is directly connected to the forex market. In fact, forex investing is a great green alternative to industrial stock or commodity investing.

FOREX HURTS NO ONE

- Unlike other financial markets, there is no 'winner' and 'loser' in forex, in other words, when we make a profit it is not coming out of someone else pocket, as currencies are always trying to reach economic equilibrium (rather than equities which are trying to constantly increase against their competition)
- There is no competition in the forex market. It is possible that all forex traders make money together
- Forex traders do not affect the market, they only provide liquidity, which is beneficial for all sides of the market

FOREX BUSINES IS ECO-FRIENDLY

- Unless legally required, forex businesses use no paper. All company documents can be stored electronically, and backed up using multiple SCSI Raid arrays, as well as on DVD
- Forex businesses create no pollution
- power requirements are only that to power computers
- Forex businesses do not contribute to the exploitation of human or natural resources

FX Living

FX is a self sustainable market. So long as the free floating currency system exists, the FX market will be a good market for business and trading. Definitely there will be demand for deliverables, trading, managed accounts, hedging by multinationals, etc.

Even in the international trading community FX seems to be a bit of a niche. Who needs FX locally? However this niche can be exploited. Also, local customers can make money by trading FX, just like if they were trading any other market.

FX Concentration

When you receive FX alerts on your Palm or mobile, what are you doing? Sleeping, eating, at work, or in a movie theater? Have any large FX trades been placed at a dinner table? Did the trader smile and wink to his dinner guest explaining how he just covered his pound shorts? If he put it like that he probably got some looks.

There is a certain level of concentration required for FX trading – it doesn't have to mimic zen buddism but definitely trading in the middle of a rock concert on your mobile is at the other end of the spectrum.

How I Got Started as a Currency Trader

I was a software engineer for 20 years before becoming a full-time Currency Trader. In 2002, I decided that working for a large corporation was not for me anymore, so I began investigating other careers. I wanted to become independent, be able to work from home, and have the potential to make a good living. I looked at several home business opportunities, and various day trading possibilities, including stocks and options, but soon discounted them all for one reason or another. I was looking for a market where large swings could take place in a short period of time, thereby maximizing my profit potential. I was also looking for a market that tended to trend more so than consolidate, once again to maximize my earning potential. I decided that trading currencies in the Forex market looked like the perfect way to achieve my goals. Since I knew very little about currency trading, I did some exhaustive research on the Internet, found a broker, then started slowly by doing a great deal of risk-free demo trading. Over the last few years, I've taken several Forex trading education courses, the best (in my opinion) being those offered by ForexInterBank, and slowly built up my confidence. I made mistakes along the way, but eventually felt confident enough to quit my job and become a full-time currency trader in October 2005. Switching from a comfortable career with a constant income to running your own business is never easy, but I'm very happy that I took the plunge. If there is one piece of advice I can offer to someone starting out as a currency trader, it would be to properly prepare yourself before risking any of your hard-earned money. Learn all you can by getting quality Forex training, find your niche in the market (short-term or long-term trades), adopt a trading method and develop a solid trading plan. Practice your trading by opening a demo account with a reputable broker, fine-tune your trading method, then open a live trading account. Most importantly, Forex trading is highly leveraged, so don't overextend yourself by risking too much of your account on any one trade.

Stay away from 4xMadeEasy software.

It is a scheme. I spent $3,200 on software and almost $7,000 on losing trade. Does not work. Class action lawsuit started against the software distributors.

Before I start, please let me apologize for impinging on your email box. You did not request this, but it I saw the post and thought that this may be helpful in some way. I hope so.

Many months ago, I was interested in 4XME based on a recommendation from a full-time trader I know. At his invitation and as his guest, I attended a one-day training seminar in Florida. I was interested in the software because the trader told me he used it in conjunction with another product we both used called "Advanced GET"; a fairly high-end trading package.

At the seminar, an "alerts" trader from PremiereFX sat next to me, which I was very happy about because I had many questions. We talked a bit and I told him that I traded full-time but didn't use their product; instead I relied GET, although I was interested in FXME.

To my surprise, he was excited to know I used GET. Here's why: he told me that is what the traders at PremiereFX use, too. Surely, I was confused. If this software, 4XME, was as good as I was being told, then why wouldn't they, the traders, use it as well? He told me the best thing about 4XME was "the money manager tool," other than that, the traders only used 4XME to match signals from GET so they could write alerts that made sense to their customers – 4XME owners – which I guess meant speaking in "4XME language" (FAS and other related terms).

Note: It should be no surprise that I never bought the product. I did test it eventually -- after finding a disgruntled customer who let me pay the signal fee for a month. The agreement was, if I figured it out, I'd purchase his 4XME. Well, I never got much out of it.

I maintained a dialogue with this PremiereFX trader, sharing with him my knowledge of GET. In time, I was invited to visit the PremiereFX offices and see their trading room. Maybe because they knew I traded full-time and used their "secret" weapon -- GET -- I wasn't perceived as a "threat" and, therefore, they had nothing to hide from me.

Interestingly, while I was there, I mentioned I still hoped to try their product. To that, the operations manager told me 4XME wasn't "very good." And he must have really believed this because in the trading room there were three monitors with GET running and only with 4XME.

I also learned that PremiereFX is an "introducing broker" for FXCM. What this means is that when 4XME customers set up a trading account at FXCM, every time they place a trade, PremiereFX gets a kickback (it's at least one pip -- or approximately $10.00).

Here's where it gets even more interesting. I learned that in November, PremiereFX had over 2000 customers -- paying an average *of $99 per month for the Alert service, which equals nearly $200,000 per month in subscription revenue. If just 10% of these customers placed one trade per day based on an alert, that equals $2,000 in one day. Again, this is based on a customer trading just one alert. I was told that the alerts generated $5000 to $40,000 a day in revenues for PremiereFX*

If you multiply this figure by 20 trading days per month, using the low-end figure, this equals $100,000 per month. Add to this $99 per month times 2000 subscribers, or $200,000, and you get a general idea of what PremiereFX was netting each month. I'm sure the figure has increased as the subscriber base has increased. The company grew from 700 alerts customers in August to 2000 in November; about 300% in three or four months. Also, I learned that in November, PremiereFX started tracking nine currency pairs (vs. the four majors they'd been focusing on) to increase revenue -- remember the "kick back." In my opinion, the sad thing is that most traders, especially new ones, should focus on no more than a couple of pairs -- more than this is confusing.

Based on the above, one might conclude the game for PremiereFX was, or is, to get their customers to trade. And they do this by issuing alerts – a lot of them. I was told that customers also trade off their "Radars" and PremiereFX management wanted their traders to issue plenty of those as well.

What is also so interesting about all of this is that Mr. Dicks, the founder of 4XME and a partner in that company, is also the owner of PremiereFX. But his traders don't trade using the product that is supposed to be so good. Also, to me, it seems a bit misleading to their alerts customers. After all, they own 4XME and probably assume the alerts traders are using the same product they are. I also find it interesting that Mr. Dicks used to work for Dynatech (sp?), the marketing company for WizeTrade and OptionsMadeEasy, which are owned by GlobalTec. I understand that Mr. Dicks brought the 4XME idea to GlobalTec -- guess he saw an opportunity and pounced. There's nothing wrong with this, excepting, of course, it's a product his very own traders don't use. Ultimately, what' does it say about it's "quality" -- it's not good enough for his staff but it is good enough for the unsuspecting?

Finally, most product guarantees are usually no less than thirty days and don't cost extra. 4XME has a 2-week guarantee that costs $500. If it's so "easy" and so able to produce profits, why the extra cost? And why only 14-days? No one has ever answered that question. Odd, don't you think?

4x Made Easy®: A Scam or Legitimate Path to Riches?

A few days ago I received an email from a reader who is participating in a 4x Made Easy® (4xME) trading group in Los Angeles. For those unfamiliar with the company offering 4xME, GlobalTec Solutions, represents itself as a Forex software, trading and training provider. Judging from the number of people who belong to Yahoo's 4xMadeEasy eGroup (8,846 members and counting), the company has succeeded in getting thousands of small investors to spend upwards of $4,200 ($3,000 up front, $99 a month thereafter) to learn how to trade the foreign exchange which, of course, is very misleading, since they're recommending their students trade with dealing desk brokers.

In my response to the gentleman who wrote me from Indian Wells, CA, I referred him to a website that posts trader reviews of brokers, education and training providers and my interest was peeked when the word "Scam" appeared in bright red letters in the column that day next to 4xMadeEasy's® name. Visiting the online reviews, I came away with the distinct impression that few have anything positive to say about the program.

After I had a couple cups of coffee this morning, curiosity got the best of me so I decided to Google "4x Made Easy"® and made a few discoveries that provide some additional perspective. The citations are old but I have no reason to believe that they are any less relevant today than they were when they were originally published.

Trading Systems: Show Me the Money

Fox 31 in Denver: Investigative Report

An Attempt to Silence a Lamb Who Thinks He Got Sheared

A visit to 4xMadeEasy.com was also informative. On their home page they provide a disclaimer toward the bottom that asserts that the company does not offer investment advice. Reading the articles above, I guess hype doesn't technically or legally qualify as "investment advice" otherwise the SEC probably would have issued a cease and desist order a long time ago.

Now if this isn't enough to convince traders to go elsewhere, get this. When you visit the company's website you'll see that they're promoting brokers who offer commission free trading which means that they are recommending that their protégés sign up to trade through one or more dealing desk brokers. No mention is made of non-dealing desk brokerage as an alternative investment platform.

Novel concept. Hype the dream of easy riches. Sell people an outlandishly expensive program that won't stand knowledgeable scrutiny and then collect a monthly fee providing useless automated signals.

I'm guessing the company will continue to prosper until 60 Minutes®

decides to do one of those wake-up-and-smell-the-coffee investigative reports they're so famous for. Until then, the principals won't have to worry about canceling their tee times because there seems to be no end to the supply of people buying into the dream of easy riches.

Is 4xMadeEasy a scam or a path to easy riches? I've pretty much made up my mind. You'll obviously have to decide for yourself.

Invitation: I would be very interested in hearing from experienced 4xMadeEasy® traders who are not only using the program but are producing the kind of no-brainer profitability the promoters lead prospective traders to believe is possible in their introductory seminar. If you are using it, how long have you been using it? Is it as easy as they would have prospects believe? If successful, how successful is it? If you felt like you got burned, I'd love to hear from you, too.[viii]

Forex for Geeks

There are a number of reasons why people who are computer literate are more likely to invest in the forex market than others. Of course, that doesn't mean that fx financial products are not offered to a plethora of clients, and many who do not even have computers will invest in FX. However, the foreign exchange markets provide opportunities not available in other markets. For example:

Investment size is irrelevant - You can invest $500 or $500 million in currency trading. Of course, the size of your account may determine the psychology of your trading strategy, but there is no reason to treat small accounts different than large accounts.

Open Source Community - Forex is more open than other markets, utilizing the fix protocol for example, or the Meta Trader platform, traders can develop their strategy without spending any money, which can be saved for their trading account. There are many open source communities of other traders and systems developers that share code, ideas, tools, and much more, through online portals like Money Tec and Strategy Builder FX.

Automated Trading - Anyone in computers at least appreciates automation. So many tasks in today's world are automated we take them for granted. Your investment accounts should also be automated. Why rely on human traders that can be

Online Business - The entire business process from account opening to trade and withdrawal, is totally online. Of course brokers and businesses have physical offices in major trading areas like New York and Chicago, but that is not a requirement. You have no real advantage being across the street from the CBOT or NYSE because there isn't any FX exchange. Also it would be quite silly to strategically place your offices near your counterparties, which are large banks -

because they are spread out all over the world. And even considering that point, those banks probably don't even house their servers in their main offices they are probably remote. As the FX market itself is decentralized from a trading point of view, it is technically as well, allowing participants of any sort to be anywhere that has a stable internet connection.

Develop your own automated system - You can start from scratch, making your own FX Strategy, and test it before using live money. Or, build on the ideas of others, tweaking settings and rules to suit your needs. It can be fun, too!

Custom tailored trading - There are very few limitations to how you can run your strategy. This makes it possible to create complex money management and trading strategies. Also, FX is traded in pairs, such as EUR/USD and EUR/CHF making calculations more dynamic (whereas most other instruments are traded against local dollars. For example if you purchase shares in Microsoft MSFT, you pay in USD.)

Ultimate software business - Think about this: Most software companies write software and then sell it. They are relying on marketing efforts more than the quality of their software, to bring in results to the bottom line. If you develop a forex trading strategy or standalone software, you are actually writing software that makes money! What better bang-for-the-buck can you have than writing a money making software?

The human element - Many people think that robotics and automation is somehow inhuman, whereas the reality is quite the opposite. Remember also, that it is humans who will be writing the software. Humans will be maintaining the servers, and many other tasks associated with automatic trading. It is not a printing press by any means, and does not absolve human traders from doing their work. More than anything, robotic trading takes out the tedious process of picking perfect entry and exit points, streamlines backtesting and analysis, and simplifies the process of portfolio building. It frees up traders time to work with clients, and don't forget it takes a lot of work to make a strategy that consistently profits.

Room for more - We saw the .com bombs of the late 90's, the day trading fad that fizzled out around 2001, and other tech start up failures. We have seen the success of Amazon and Yahoo, which really are not all that revolutionary. Although it is convenient to shop at Amazon, didn't we have mail order catalogs in the 80's? We have not seen much development in the investment and trading industry, which could be a very profitable business to be in. Of course, it's impossible to convince any industrialist of the potential for profit, but many programmers have taken up forex strategy development as a part time hobby and have made many strategies that are successful. There is room for more participants in the FX market, and they do not compete. If someone makes a strategy that is better than mine, I am a likely investor in that strategy. There isn't the kind of competition that exists in traditional I.T. business.

Chapter 6: The Electronic Revolution

The Electronic Revolution: Forex begins post .com

Uncorrelated to the forex market, the past 20 years the global economy has been in the process of automation and digitization of all aspects of business and life. Computers are making our lives simpler and more complex at the same time. How simpler? Now, you don't have to write checks every month, mail them, and worry about balancing your account. You can automatically pay your bills with Internet banking, which has low fees, and if setup properly is fully automatic. How more complex? Research is at your fingertips. Business intelligence equals as much time as you are willing to spend in front of the computer and Internet. Anyone in a garage can start a company with a website, telephone, and computer. New technology equals new challenges, as the pre-industrial society faced basic challenges such as transportation and manufacturing processes; we now face an energy crises to power our machines, while at the same time the internet is shaping how corporations and governments operate.

This paradigm shift is creating a new face of players, and clients. It seems unheard of that a client or trader of forex doesn't have a computer, but they do exist. Different types of people are attracted to forex than to oil investing for example.

Computers are changing the way we live, invest, and bank. You can trade your own money, or watch live how your account is doing. Electronically you can download account statements, cancel your account, anything. In fact, the entire customer life cycle is fully automated, assuming the customer never picks up the phone.

The division between customers and account representatives is also blurring, just as retail is being ruined by companies like Amazon.com. Why should you pay 20% more for something? Why should a large company hire thousands of people to promote FX accounts that market themselves?

Automation cuts costs, thus cutting the need for humans. This in turn shapes the technology that drives the development of further automation, and so on. For example, if you have a fully automatic FX brokerage, what are you supposed to do all day? You will likely sit around your home office or private island and think about trading strategies – or you won't think at all. Most likely you will NOT be violating NFA rules, harassing customers, advertising on CNN, or causing trouble in general.

Now, psychotic business behavior is a pure choice. There is no reason to sue people, lie to customers, steal, etc. It's all possible and all automatic with electronic investing, trading, and banking. These 3 things represent an example customer lifecycle:

1.	A customer accumulates funds in an account by selling his goods and services

2.	A customer needs to invest that money somewhere

3.	Funds are invested, and traded

4.	Customer receives a profit (or loss) and finally banks his funds, probably in an account with an electronic link, in the future in a currency other than physical (such as e-gold)

None of this would have been possible 20 years ago, and the electronic revolution is shaping not only the way FX companies do business, but the FX market dynamics themselves.

Programmers replace traders

The classic trader is 6'3", fit, well educated, good looking, wealthy, charming, debonair gentleman. The classic programmer is socially detached, usually intelligent, obsessive about computers (like I suppose traders are obsessive about making money or watches), and definitely not interested in 'trading'. But what the market now comes down to is automated systems – whether they be strategy systems or automated pass through execution systems, there is a degree of control each must have (trader & programmer). For example you can't just pay a programmer to rewrite the banking system – he has to have a small understanding of how the system works. But if programmers are recoding and automating financial markets, what the hell do we need traders for? In fact, what do we need the wealthy for? Uh-oh, scary concepts are happening behind the scenes. Who understands this crap? Fire him!

FX Business problem

Typically FX is a secretive business that takes place behind NDA's and long legal contracts. This fairly protects traders who develop FX trading systems – there is a separation between marketing, trading, business, etc. But what do you put on a website about your program, where do you draw the line? It's clear there is a divide between established financial firms and webmasters who can be anyone, anywhere. The Internet market place has no rules per say – it's a no holds barred; most hits take all, no rules, offshore server, bloodbath. A business website can be copied in less than an hour – as long as it takes to download, 'global search and replace' the domain to another URL, and re-uploaded with the logo.gif replaced with my-logo.gif using a domain name similar to but not exactly what it just copied.

77

90% of the people in this online game are not even in FX business, they are webmasters, or SEO gurus who have smelled money in FX. Either way, it's an unregulated market, as you can host servers offshore and not be subject to NFA of FSA compliance.

Internet Dwellers

There are 2 sides to the FX community – there is the establishment, which is the historical business community since FX market began trading – and the new internet community. The 2 are clearly on other planets, and with good reason. Some FX dealers don't have a computer! Conversely, some internet 'FX businessmen' have never been to school, have never even traded 1 euro! I mean it's possible to purchase FXtrading.com and open an FX website, offer FX services, with absolutely no scrutiny of the government or regulatory bodies. Here is where deregulated FX works against itself – the proliferation of uneducated mentally disturbed webmasters who promulgate lies and misinformation such as promoting managed accounts that make 10% - 50% per month, consistently, for the past 10 years.

The lack of information and homework on the part of some of them is scary. Whether they intend to defraud or are just plain lost in space, is up for debate BUT irrelevant – they are still the proliferators of propaganda which hurts the community as a whole.

New Paradigm

How fragile the world has become, when you can unplug a network connection that knocks off the connection between the bank and the data center server. Will those who have been building these networks be around in 20 years to service them? Will the declining demand for I.T. And I.Q. Keep up with an ever increasing demand for service? How will I.T. And M.I.S. Handle global warming, a changing energy regime, increasing solar flares, and a demand for more regulation from industrialists?

Interbank FX Announces $40 Million Investment by Spectrum Equity Investors

SALT LAKE CITY, July 19, 2007-- Interbank FX, a leading provider of online foreign exchange trading, announced today that it has received a $40 million minority equity investment from Spectrum Equity Investors. The investment supports Interbank FX's agency-execution business model and proprietary technologies, and will further position the company for its next stage of growth. Interbank FX management will retain full operating authority of the company, and there will be no changes to the firm's strategy, operations, personnel or commitment to customer service. Additional terms of the transaction were not disclosed.

Todd Crosland, founder and CEO of Interbank FX, said, "We are extremely pleased to have Spectrum Equity make this strategic investment in the company, and believe this partnership will help Interbank FX achieve its goal of becoming the premier forex trading platform in the marketplace. With their domain expertise and financial resources, Spectrum represents the ideal partner to help Interbank FX capitalize on the tremendous growth opportunities facing the company and to assist our continued innovation in establishing market-leading execution and service offerings."

"Since inception, Interbank FX has distinguished itself as an industry leader with its 'no dealing desk,' agency-execution business model and customer service focus," said Vic Parker, managing director of Spectrum Equity Investors. "We are excited to be involved in the next stage of the company's development. Interbank FX is a perfect fit for Spectrum, given our firm's experience in technology-enabled financial services, risk management, compliance and online services, as well as our investment focus on rapidly growing, profitable services companies."

"As a result of tremendous growth in online spot forex trading, we have evaluated numerous investment opportunities in this sector over the last five years," said Chris Mitchell, managing director of Spectrum Equity Investors. "We believe Interbank FX represents a unique opportunity to back an accomplished and high-integrity management team in conjunction with an agency-only trading execution model in which company interests are squarely aligned with those of its customers. We believe this alignment will enable Interbank FX to continue the empowerment of its customers via price transparency and industry-leading trading spreads."

About Spectrum Equity Investors

Spectrum Equity Investors is a private equity firm with over $4 billion of capital under management. It partners with management teams of growing companies in information and technology-enabled service industries and helps them develop industry-leading franchises. Select portfolio companies include R.J. O'Brien, the largest independent futures brokerage in the United States; RiskMetrics Group, a leading global provider of risk management analytics and research; Arrowhead General Insurance Agency, the largest private multi-line general agent and program specialist in the insurance industry; World-Check, a leading provider of Know Your Customer (KYC) and Anti-Money Laundering (AML) database information; Net Quote, the largest online source of consumer leads to the insurance industry; and Demand Media, a leading provider of website registration, optimization and monetization services. For more information about Spectrum, visit www.spectrumequity.com.

About Interbank FX

Interbank FX (www.interbankfx.com) is a Futures Commission Merchant (FCM), registered with the Commodity Futures Trading Commission and a member of the National Futures Association (NFA). Interbank FX offers individual traders, fund managers and institutional customers proprietary technology and tools to trade spot foreign exchange online and via wireless devices. Customers execute directly from a streaming quote feed, not from a dealing desk that trades against its customers, and the majority of company revenues are generated by a transparent agency-based spread on transactions. Through Interbank FX's partnership with leading worldwide institutions, traders have access to liquidity in micro-, mini- and standard lots sizes with one click execution. Interbank FX is committed to maintaining a high standard of service that enables customers to focus on trading opportunities in the forex market while managing transaction margin and liquidity risks. Interbank FX has over 17,000 customer accounts in more than 135 countries. Trading in the off-exchange retail foreign currency market is one of the riskiest forms of investing and should only be attempted by experienced traders.

Wiki Movement

Normally, it would take considerable energy to cite and properly credit sources. But with the wiki movement, we have a fine-tuned open source information portal at our fingertips. How can we fight it?

Wikipedia (IPA: [/□w□ki□pi□di.□/] or [/□wiki-/]) is a global and multilingual Web-based cooperative free-content encyclopedia. It exists as a wiki, a type of website that allows visitors to edit its content; the word Wikipedia itself is a portmanteau of wiki and encyclopedia and is often abbreviated to **WP** by its users. Wikipedia is written collaboratively by volunteers, allowing most articles to be changed by anyone with access to a computer, web browser and Internet connection.

The project began on January 15, 2001 as a complement to the expert-written (and now defunct) Nupedia, and is now operated by the non-profit Wikimedia Foundation. Wikipedia has more than 3,800,000 articles in many languages, including more than 1,145,000 in the English-language version. Since its inception, Wikipedia has steadily risen in popularity[1] and has spawned several sister projects.

Wikipedia's most notable style policy is that editors are required to uphold a "neutral point of view", under which notable perspectives are summarized without an attempt to determine an objective truth.

Wikipedia's co-founder, Jimmy Wales, has called Wikipedia "an effort to create and distribute a multilingual free encyclopedia of the highest possible quality to every single person on the planet in their own language."[2] However, there has been controversy over Wikipedia's reliability and accuracy, with the site receiving criticism for its susceptibility to vandalism, uneven quality and inconsistency, systemic bias, and preference of consensus or popularity over credentials. Nevertheless, its free distribution, constant updates, diverse and detailed coverage, and numerous multilingual versions have made it one of the most-used reference resources available on the Internet.

There are over 200 language editions of Wikipedia, around 130 of which are active. Fourteen editions have more than 50,000 articles each: English (the original), German, French, Polish, Japanese, Dutch, Italian, Swedish, Portuguese, Spanish, Russian, Chinese, Norwegian and Finnish. Its German-language edition has been distributed on DVD-ROM, and there are also proposals for an English DVD or paper edition. Many of its other editions are mirrored or have been forked by other websites.

From the copyright page

The license Wikipedia uses grants free access to our content in the same sense as free software is licensed freely. This principle is known as copyleft. That is to say, Wikipedia content can be copied, modified, and redistributed *so long as* the new version grants the same freedoms to others and acknowledges the authors of the Wikipedia article used (a direct link back to the article satisfies our author credit requirement). Wikipedia articles therefore will remain free forever and can be used by anybody subject to certain restrictions, most of which serve to ensure that freedom.

To fulfill the above goals, the text contained in Wikipedia is licensed to the public under the GNU Free Documentation License (GFDL). The full text of this license is at Wikipedia:Text of the GNU Free Documentation License.

Open Source

Open source describes practices in production and development that promote access to the end product's sources. Some consider it as a philosophy, and others consider it as a pragmatic methodology. Before *open source* became widely adopted, developers and producers used a variety of phrases to describe the concept; the term *open source* gained popularity with the rise of the Internet and its enabling of diverse production models, communication paths, and interactive communities.[1] Subsequently, open source software became the most prominent face of open source.

The open source model can allow for the concurrent use of different agendas and approaches in production, in contrast with more centralized models of development such as those typically used in commercial software companies.[2]

History

Those involved with journalism and open source intelligence used the earliest known practices of open source that focused on accessibility rather than modification of sources. Software developers used to commonly release their code under public domain until they wanted to control how such freely accessible sources are modified and distributed. Developers, like the Free Software Foundation, began to license their work, but they still kept it as free software.

The "open source" label came out of a strategy session[3] held at Palo Alto in reaction to Netscape's January 1998 announcement of a source code release for Navigator. The group of individuals at the session included Christine Peterson who suggested "open source" and also included Todd Anderson, Larry Augustin, John Hall, Sam Ockman, and Eric S. Raymond. They used the opportunity before the release of Navigator's source code to clarify a potential confusion caused by the ambiguity of the word free in English, so that the perception of free software is not anti-commercial. Netscape listened and released their code as open source under the name of Mozilla.

This milestone may be commonly seen as the birth of the open source movement. However, earlier researchers with access to the Advanced Research Projects Agency Network (ARPANET) used a process called Request for Comments, which is similar to open standards, to develop telecommunication network protocols. Characterized by contemporary open source work, this collaborative process led to the birth of the Internet in 1969.

The Open Source Initiative formed in February 1998 by Eric S. Raymond and Bruce Perens. With at about 20 years of evidence from case histories of closed development versus open development already provided by the Internet, the OSI continued to present the 'open source' case to commercial businesses. They sought to bring a higher profile to the practical benefits of freely available source code, and they wanted to bring major software businesses and other high-tech industries into open source. Bruce Perens adapted Debian's Free Software Guidelines to make the Open Source Definition. [4]

Critics have said that the term "open source" fosters an ambiguity of a different kind such that it confuses the mere availability of the source with the freedom to use, modify, and redistribute it. Developers have used the term Free/Open-Source Software (FOSS), or Free/Libre/Open-Source Software (FLOSS), consequently, to describe open-source software that is freely available and free of charge.

Markets

Software is not the only field affected by open source; many fields of study and social and political views have been affected by the growth of the concept of open source. Advocates in one field will often support the expansion of open source in other fields, including Linus Torvalds who is quoted as saying, "the future is open source everything."

The open source movement has been the inspiration for increased transparency and liberty in other fields, including the release of biotechnology research by CAMBIA, Wikipedia, and other projects. The open-source concept has also been applied to media other than computer programs, e.g., by Creative Commons. It also constitutes an example of user innovation (see for example the book Democratizing Innovation). Often, open source is an expression where it simply means that a system is available to all who wish to work on it.

Agriculture

- Beverages
- OpenCola — An idea inspired by the open source movement. Soft drink giants like Coke and Pepsi hold their formulas as closely guarded secrets. Now volunteers have posted the recipe for a similar cola drink on the Internet. The taste is said to be comparable to that of the standard beverages.
- Beer — A beer recipe called Vores Øl. Following its release, an article in Wired magazine commented that "as open source spreads beyond software to online encyclopedias like Wikipedia and biological research, it was only a matter of time before somebody created an open-source beer".[5] The beer was created by students at the IT-University in Copenhagen together with Superflex, a Copenhagen-based artist collective, to illustrate how open source concepts might be applied outside the digital world. The likewise concept expands upon a statement found in the Free Software Definition: "Free software is a matter of liberty, not price. To understand the concept, you should think of 'free' as in 'free speech' not as in 'free beer.'"[6]

Content

- Open-content projects organized by the Wikimedia Foundation — Sites such as Wikipedia and Wiktionary have embraced the open-content GFDL and Creative Commons content licenses. These licenses were designed to adhere to principles similar to various open-source software development licenses. Many of these licenses ensure that content remains free for re-use, that source documents are made readily available to interested parties, and that changes to content are accepted easily back into the system. Some have noted that the Wikipedia editorial process is similar to the bazaar-style development process described in Eric Raymond's essay, The Cathedral and the

Bazaar.

Health

- Medicine

Pharmaceuticals — There have been several proposals for open-source pharmaceutical development, such as the article Finding Cures for Tropical Diseases: Is Open Source an Answer?, which led to the establishment of the Tropical Disease Initiative. There are also a number of not-for-profit "virtual pharmas" such as the Institute for One World Health and the Drugs for Neglected Diseases Initiative.

Technology

- Computer software
- Open source software — software whose source code is published and made available to the public, enabling anyone to copy, modify and redistribute the source code without paying royalties or fees. Open source code evolves through community cooperation. These communities are composed of individual programmers as well as very large companies. Some examples of open source initiatives are Linux, Eclipse, Apache, Tomcat web server, Moodle, Mozilla, Mediawiki (the software that runs Wikipedia), and various other projects hosted on SourceForge and elsewhere.

- Computer hardware
- Open source hardware — hardware whose initial specification, usually in a software format, are published and made available to the public, enabling anyone to copy, modify and redistribute the hardware and source code without paying royalties or fees. Open source hardware evolves through community cooperation. These communities are composed of individual hardware/software developers, hobbyists, as well as very large companies. An example of Open Source Hardware initiatives are: Sun Microsystem's OpenSPARC T1 Multicore processor. Sun states in their Press release: "The source code will be released under an Open Source Initiative (OSI)-approved open source license."

- Open design — which involves applying open source methodologies to the design of artifacts and systems in the physical world. Very nascent but has huge potential.

- Teaching - which involves applying the concepts of open source to instruction using a shared web space as a platform to improve upon learning, organizational, and management challenges.

Society and culture

Open source as applied to culture defines a culture in which fixations are made generally available. Participants in such an open source

84

culture are able to modify those products, if needed, and redistribute them back into the community or other organizations.

Government

• Open source government — **primarily** refers to use of open source software and technologies in traditional government organizations and government operations such as voting.
• Open source politics — is a term used to describe a political process that uses Internet technologies such as blogs and email to provide for a rapid feedback mechanism between political organizations and their supporters. There is also an alternative conception of the term which relates to the development of public policy under a set of rules and processes similar to the Open Source Software movement.
• Open source governance — is similar to open source politics, but it applies more to the democratic process and promotes the freedom of information.

Media

• Open source journalism — referred to the standard journalistic techniques of news gathering and fact checking, and reflected a similar term that was in use from 1992 in military intelligence circles, open source intelligence. It is now commonly used to describe forms of innovative publishing of online journalism, rather than the sourcing of news stories by a professional journalist.

• OpenDocument — An open document file format for saving and exchanging editable office documents such as text documents (including memos, reports, and books), spreadsheets, charts, and presentations. Organizations and individuals that store their data in an open format such as OpenDocument avoid being locked in to a single software vendor, leaving them free to switch software if their current vendor goes out of business, raises their prices, changes their software, or changes their licensing terms to something less favorable.

• Creative Commons — A non-profit organization devoted to expand the range of creative work available for others legally to build upon and share.

• Open source movie production - Either an open call system in which a changing crew and cast collaborate in movie production or a system in which the end result is made available for re-use by others or in which exclusively open source products are used in the production.

• Open source documentary - A documentary film whose production process involves the open contributions of archival material, footage, and other filmic elements, both in unedited and

85

edited form. By doing so, on-line contributors become part of the process of creating the film, helping to influence the editorial and visual material to be used in the documentary, as well as its themeatic development. The first open source documentary, "The American Revolution" is currently in production.

Innovation Communities

• Open Source concepts and structures can be used to organize communities. At <u>Bootstrap Austin</u>, an open source community, entrepreneurs provide negotiated products/services at no cost to the group. The entrepreneur benefits by gaining reputation in the community, experience and an improved product. The community is at once a customer and Evangelist for the product/service. The entrepreneur monetizes their product or service outside the Bootstrap community.

Chapter7: Origins of Money and FX

Money

Contrary to popular belief, the real conspiracy behind the world banking elite is mass stupidity of the public consumer. One school of thought claims that throughout history, the world's ruling powers have used the money system to control the poor: the common division between the haves, and the have-nots. This is however a poor excuse of lazy unmotivated victims of this system. The reality is there has never been an adopted elegant solution that solves the most basic of economic issues: how to value trade.

Any system, even a theoretical flawless system, is subject to human error, greed, stupidity, emotion, etc. This causes the systems, however great, to eventually fail.

Banks are doing consumers a great service by offering many of the account types they do. Of course there are borderline, questionable high-risk lending practices, for example, which are questionably ethical. But this exists in any field, such as in forex, where you have many ethical and stable institutions, and a few rogue cowboys who don't respect the rules of the game.

FX Primary Mover

If you open an FX account, and turn $300 into $3000 – where did the money come from? Since currency is valued only in terms of other currency and never in absolute value, it is mathematically possible that all players in the FX market win – or at least the majority. This is NOT the case in other markets, which are bubble-based. When you are creating profits in an FX account, it is similar to the process of the fed creating money supply. That money did not exist before, but now that it does, you can withdraw it and spend it in the real world.

Cybermoney

There is 9million (in USD terms) in e-gold right now. As the price of gold shoots past 600 USD, the same e-gold still exists but its value in USD is greater – giving you larger purchasing power in USD but THE SAME in e-gold (for vendors who price in e-gold). Still, 9 million dollars is not a lot of money – it's the price of an office building in a small city.

Parallels – coincidence?

The FX market *affects* the economy more than any other.

What effects does FX have on your life?

Hollywood creates blockbuster movies with special FX, the money masters could create no better FX in world finance than FX. Truly, FX has an appropriate dual meaning.

If you are a poor trader and lose all your money, and are broke, you then can become a *broker*.

Money

From Wikipedia, the free encyclopedia

An example of **Money**. More specifically, Brazilian Real bills and coins.

"Money", is any good or token used by a society as a medium of exchange, store of value and unit of account.

Trade without money more often than not is the direct bartering of one commodity for another. Bartering is often inefficient because it requires a coincidence of wants between traders. The emergence of some form of money is a natural market phenomenon observed repeatedly across civilisations and is not dependent on any central authority or government. Indeed, the division of labour in any but the most basic of forms cannot occur without it.

Commodity money was amongst the earliest forms of money to emerge. Under a commodity money system, the object used as money has inherent value. It is usually adopted to simplify transactions in a barter economy; thus it functions first as a medium of exchange. It quickly begins functioning as a store of value, since holders of perishable goods can easily convert them into durable money. In modern economies, commodity money has also been used as a unit of account. Gold-backed currency notes are a common derivative form of commodity money.

Fiat money is a relatively modern invention. A central authority (government) creates a new money object that has negligible inherent value. The widespread acceptance of fiat money is most frequently enhanced by the central authority mandating the money's acceptance under penalty of law and demanding this money in payment of taxes or tribute. At various times in history government issued promissory notes have later become fiat currencies (e.g. US Dollar) and fiat currencies have gone on to become a form of commodity currency (e.g.Swiss Dinar).

History of money

Main article: History of money

Money has developed over the years from the likes of conch shells to requiring management by sophisticated international banking systems. From 550 BC, accepting salt from a person in Roman times was synonymous with drawing a salary, taking pay, or being in that person's service.

The history of money has generally seen commodity money replaced by more formal systems, as money has been progressively brought under the control of governments.

Essential characteristics of money

Money has all of the following three characteristics:

1. It must be a medium of exchange

When an object is consistently used as an intermediate object of trade, as opposed to direct barter, then it is regarded as a medium of exchange. The utility of such an object in simplifying the process of trade leads to direct demand for the object.

Either coercion or faith is necessary in order for a single object to become or to remain dominant in this function.

When people are coerced to use or, alternatively, they trust an object and demand it in order to exchange and trade, then this object is considered money.

2. It must be a unit of account

When the value of a market good is frequently used to measure or compare the value of other goods or where its value is used to denominate debts then it is functioning as a unit of account.

A debt or an IOU can not serve as a unit of account because its value is specified by comparison to some external reference value, some actual unit of account that may be used for settlement. Unless, of course, the debt or IOU is also an accepted medium of exchange, in which case we have money.

For example, if in some culture people are inclined to measure the worth of things with reference to goats then we would regard goats as the dominant unit of account in that culture. For instance we may say that today a horse is worth 10 goats and a good hut is worth 45 goats. We would also say that an IOU denominated in goats would change value at much the same rate as real goats.

3. It must be a store of value

When an object is purchased primarily to store value for future trade then it is being used as a store of value. For example, a sawmill might maintain an inventory of lumber that has market value. Likewise it might keep a cash box that has some currency that holds market value. Both would represent a store of value because through trade they can be reliably converted to other goods at some future date. Most non-perishable goods have this quality.

Many goods or tokens have some of the characteristics outlined above. However no good or token is money unless it can satisfy all three criteria.

Credit as money

Credit is often loosely referred to as money. However credit only satisfies items one and three of the above "Essential Characteristics of Money" criteria. Credit completely fails criterion number two. Hence to be strictly accurate credit is a money substitute and not money proper.

This distinction between money and credit causes much confusion in discussions of monetary theory. In lay terms, and when convenient in academic discussion, credit and money are frequently used interchangeably. For example bank deposits are generally included in summations of the national broad money supply. However any detailed study of monetary theory needs to recognize the proper distinction between money and credit.

The rest of this article frequently uses the term money in the looser sense of the word.

Desirable features of money

To function as money, the monetary item should possess a number of features:

To be a medium of exchange**:**

• It should have liquidity, easily tradable, with a low spread between the prices to buy and sell
• It should be easily transportable; precious metals have a high value to weight ratio. This is why oil, coal, vermiculite, or water are

not suitable as money even though they are valuable. Paper notes have proved highly convenient in this regard.

• It should have a low transaction cost while being used to offer a cost advantage over bartering.

To be a unit of account**:**

• It should be divisible into small units without destroying its value; precious metals can be coined from bars, or melted down into bars again. This is why leather, or live animals are not suitable as money.

• It should be fungible: that is, one unit or piece must be exactly equivalent to another, which is why diamonds, works of art or real estate are not suitable as money.

• It must be a specific weight, or measure, to be verifiably countable.

To be a store of value**:**

• It should be long lasting, durable, it must not be perishable or subject to decay. This is why food items, expensive spices, or even fine silks or oriental rugs, are not generally suitable as money.

• It should have a stable value; a value intrinsic in itself, such as a luxury item, scarce, or rare.

• It should be difficult to counterfeit, and the genuine must be easily recognizable. These reasons are why paper, or electronic credits, are often not desirable as money.

For these reasons, gold and silver have been chosen again and again throughout history as money in more societies and in more cultures and over longer time periods than any other items.

One key benefit of these features of money is that it facilitates and encourages trade; because barter is inefficient.

Modern forms of money

Banknotes (also known as paper money) and coins are the most liquid forms of tangible money and are commonly used for small person-to-person transactions. Today, Gold is commonly used as a store of value, but is not directly used as a medium of exchange and thus is no longer a form of money.

There are also less tangible forms of money, which nevertheless serve the same functions as money. Checks, debit cards and wire transfers are used as means to more easily transfer larger amounts of money between bank accounts. Electronic money is an entirely non-physical currency that is traded and used over the internet.

Economics of money

Money is one of the most central topics studied in economics and forms its most cogent link to finance. Monetarism is an economic theory which predominantly deals with the supply and demand for money.

Monetary policy aims to manage the money supply, inflation and interest to affect output and employment. Inflation is the decrease in the value of a specific currency over time and can be caused by dramatic increases in the money supply. The interest rate, the cost of borrowing money, is an important tool used to control inflation and economic growth in monetary economics. Central banks are often made responsible for monitoring and controlling the money supply, interest rates and banking.

A monetary crisis can have very significant economic effects, particularly if it leads to monetary failure and the adoption of a much less efficient barter economy. This happened in Russia, for instance, after the fall of the Soviet Union.

There have been many historical arguments regarding the combination of money's functions, some arguing that they need more separation and that a single unit is insufficient to deal with them all. Financial capital is a more general and inclusive term for all liquid instruments, whether or not they are a uniformly recognized tender.

Private currencies

Main article: Private currency

In many countries, the issue of private paper currencies has been severely restricted by law.

A private 1 dollar note, issued by the "Delaware Bridge Company" of New Jersey 1836-1841.

In the United States, the Free Banking Era lasted between 1837 and

1866. States, municipalities, private banks, railroad and construction companies, stores, restaurants, churches and individuals printed an estimated 8,000 different monies by 1860. If the issuer went bankrupt, closed, left town, or otherwise went out of business the note would be worthless. Such organizations earned the nickname of "wildcat banks" for a reputation of unreliability and that they were often situated in far-off, unpopulated locales that were said to be more apt to wildcats than people. On the other hand, according to Lawrence H. White's article in The Freeman: Ideas on Liberty - October 1993 *"it turns out that "wildcat" banking is largely a myth. Although stories about crooked banking practices are entertaining—and for that reason have been repeated endlessly by textbooks—modern economic historians have found that there were in fact very few banks that fit any reasonable definition of wildcat bank."* The National Bank Act of 1863 ended the "wildcat bank" period.

In Australia, the Bank Notes Tax Act of 1910 basically shut down the circulation of private currencies by imposing a prohibitive tax on the practice. Many other nations have similar such policies that eliminate private sector competition.

In Scotland and Northern Ireland private sector banks are licensed to print their own paper money by the government. These are known as currency notes and are only accepted as currency in the jurisdiction where they were issued.

Today privately issued electronic money is in circulation. Some of these private currencies are backed by historic forms of money such as gold, as in the case of digital gold currency. Transactions in these currencies represent an annual turnover value in billions of US dollars.

It is possible for privately issued money to be backed by any other material, although some people argue about perishable materials. After all, gold, or platinum, or silver, have in some regards less utility than previously (their electrical properties notwithstanding), while currency backed by energy (measured in joules) or by transport (measured in kilogramme*kilometre/hour) or by food [1] is also possible and may be accepted by the people, if legalised. It is important to understand though that, as long as money is above all an agreement to use something as a medium of exchange, it is up to a community (or to whoever holds the power within a community) to decide whether money should be backed by whatever material or should be totally virtual

Money supply

Main article: Money supply

The money supply is the amount of money available within a specific economy available for purchasing goods or services. The supply is usually considered as four escalating categories M0, M1, M2 and M3. The categories grow in size with M3 representing all forms of money (including credit) and M0 being just base money (coins, bills, and central bank deposits). M0 is also money that can satisfy private banks' reserve requirements. In the United States, the Federal Reserve is responsible for controlling the money supply, while in the Euro area the respective institution is the ECB. Other central banks with greater impact on global finances are the Bank of Japan, People's Bank of China and the Bank of England.

Growing the money supply

Historically money was a metal (gold, silver, etc,) or other object that was difficult to duplicate, but easy to transport and divide. Later it consisted of paper notes, now issued by all modern governments. With the rise of modern industrial capitalism it has gone through several phases including but not limited to:

1.   Bank notes - paper issued by banks as an interest-bearing loan. (These were common in the 19th century but not seen anymore.)
2.   Paper notes, coins with varying amounts of precious metal (usually called legal tender) issued by various governments. There is also a near-money in the form of interest bearing bonds issued by governments with solid credit ratings.
3.   Bank credit through the creation of chequable deposits in the granting of various loans to business, government and individuals. (It is critical that we understand that when a bank makes a loan, that is *new* money and when a loan is paid off that money is destroyed. Only the interest paid on it remains.)

Thus, all debt denominated in dollars -- mortgages, money markets, credit card debt, travelers cheques -- is money. However, the creation of dollar-denominated debt (or any generic obligation) only creates money when a bank (as opposed to a credit card company) is granting the debt. "High powered" money (M0) is created when the elected government spends money into the economy. The money created in the bank loan process is bank money and these two forms of money trade at par one with the other. Banks are limited in the amount of loans they can grant and thus in the amount of bank money (credit) they can create by both the net assets of the bank and by reserve requirements (M0). For most intents and purposes the aggregate of M0 multiplied by the reserve requirement will be an indicator of (but this is somewhat greater than) the aggregate of loans. If additional money is needed in the banking system to allow more loans the

Federal Reserve will create money by purchasing Bonds or T-bills with money created from the other. No matter who sells the bonds the money will end up in the banking system as M0. The Fed could purchase lolly pops if that would accomplish the purpose of expansion better than a purchase of Bonds.

Shrinking the money supply (M3)

Perhaps the most obvious way money can be destroyed is if paper bills are burned or taken out of circulation by the central bank. But, it should be remembered that legal tender usually constitutes less than 4% of the broad money supply.

Another way money can be destroyed is when any bank loan is paid off or any government bond or T-Bill is purchased by the private sector. The money value of the contract or bond is destroyed — taken out of circulation. If a bank loan is defaulted upon then the "interest" paid by other borrowers will be employed to cover the default. A very large part of the "interest" paid on bank loans is actually a finance charge employed to cover bad loans. The group of good borrowers pay the loan instead of the original borrower. In cases where the default is huge such as loans to foreign governments Fed intervention has, in the past, rescued the banks. In this instance it would seem that the taxpayers and/or money holders (savers) will pay the debt. The effects on the money supply will be controlled, again, by the level of bond purchase or redemption or the level of T-Bill sales or purchases by the Treasury.

Money can be destroyed if savers withdraw funds from a bank, in which case that money can no longer be used for lending. Bank savings are actually a kind of loans — savers loan their money to a bank at a low interest rate or merely in exchange for the benefit of convenience or its security (accepting that they lose a small amount of value to inflation). The bank may use this loan to manage its liabilities (its deposit liabilities created by loans). It must be recalled that the federal reserve banking system is *mostly* a closed system. A check written on bank A gets deposited in Bank B and a check written on bank B gets deposited in Bank C and a check on bank C gets deposited in bank A. At the end of the day the bankers go have a beer and see who needs to borrow from whom:) On a good day very little borrowing needs to be done because a bank gets as much in new deposits as it does in paid out funds. Even if a bank is short of reserves it can borrow the reserves from another bank at the *discount* rate.

In extreme forms, a bank run or panic may drive a bank into insolvency and, if uninsured, the savings of all its depositors are lost. Such bank failures were a major cause of the tremendous contraction in the money supply that occurred during the Great Depression, particularly in the United States. In that country many banking reforms were subsequently enacted during the New Deal, including the creation of the Federal Deposit Insurance Corporation to guarantee private bank deposits.

Slang words and synonyms associated with money

Some money

- Dosh
- Cash
- Bucks
- Spondulix
- Dough
- Bread
- Silver
- The quids
- Nickels
- Coppers
- Dime
- Shrapnel (when refering to coins)

My money

- Slice of my pie
- My stack
- My wedge

Amounts of money

- Grand = 1,000 currency units
- Ten-er = 10 currency units
- Five-er = 5 currency units
- Quid = £1
- Buck = $1

An Experiment in Worgl

The year was 1932; the world was gripped by the greatest economic depression that it had ever known. One man in a small town decided to try something new to help the people of his community. In doing so the town made economic history. The town was Worgl in the Bavarian province of Germany. To understand the Worgl experiment you have to understand the man behind it. The towns mayor Michael Unterguggenberger.

Michael Unterguggenberger

Michael was born into an old Tyrolean peasant family. He lived the life of a poor European without falling into the mental trap of heavy blue-collar work. He apprenticed himself to a master mechanic. After apprenticeship he became a journeyman mechanic. At the age of twenty-one he had his first post at the Worgl railway station. His striving for social justice jeopardized his personal advancement. In taking a stand for his fellow workers as a trade union man, he was not promoted any higher. In 1912 he was elected representative for the union of Innsbruck Rail Engineers in the committee for personnel. Yet to the officials of the Austrian Railroad network he was seen as the person who represented the concerns of the workers against the moneyed interests of the railroad. Later Alex von Muralt would write that Michael Unterguggenberger always stressed that he was not a Marxist.

Wörgl

Worgl was a small town that had grown rapidly in the early 1900's. Then came the crash of 1929, which quickly spread, into Europe. Michael was town councilor, he soon became deputy mayor. In 1931 he was elected mayor of Worgl. As mayor he had a long list of projects he wanted to accomplish. Projects like repaving roads, street lighting, extending water distribution across the entire town and planting trees along the streets. But in the midst of the depression out of the towns population of 4,500, 1,500 were without a job and 200 families were penniless.

Silvio Gesell

Michael read and re-read "The Natural Order" by Silvio Gesell. He

97

talked with people in the town and convinced the members of the Worgl Welfare Committee to hold a session on July 5, 1932. In this session he gave a short summary and then proposed a "Distress Relief Program". He stated that slow circulation of money is the principal cause of the faltering economy. Money as a medium of exchange increasingly vanished out of working people's hands and accumulates into the hands of the few who collect interest and do not return it back to the market. He proposed that in Worgl the slow-circulating National Bank currency would be replaced by "Certified Compensation Bills". The council would issue the Bills and the public would accept the Bills for their full nominal value. Bills would be issued in the denominations of 1, 5 and 10 shillings. A total issue of 32,000 Worgl "Money Bills" was printed and put into circulation.

Worgl Money

On July 31, 1932 the town administrator purchased the first lot of Bills from the Welfare Committee for a total face value of 1,800 Schillings and used it to pay wages. These first wages paid out were returned to the community on almost the same day as tax payments. By the third day it was thought that the Bills had been counterfeited because the 1000 Schillings issued had already accounted for 5,100 Schillings in unpaid taxes. Michael Unterguggenberger knew better, the velocity of money had increased and his Worgl money was working.

Worgl money was a stamp script money. The Worgl Bills would depreciate 1% of their nominal value monthly. To prevent this devaluation the owner of the Bill must affix a stamp the value of which is the devaluation on the last day of the month. Stamps were purchased at the parish hall. Because nobody wanted to pay a devaluation (hoarding) fee the Bills were spent as fast as possible.

The reverse side of the Bills were printed with the following declaration: "To all whom it may concern ! Sluggishly circulating money has provoked an unprecedented trade depression and plunged millions into utter misery. Economically considered, the destruction of the world has started. - It is time, through determined and intelligent action, to endeavour to arrest the downward plunge of the trade machine and thereby to save mankind from fratricidal wars, chaos, and dissolution. Human beings live by exchanging their services. Sluggish circulation has largely stopped this exchange and thrown millions of willing workers out of employment. - We must therefore revive this exchange of services and by its means bring the unemployed back to the ranks of the producers. Such is the object of the labour certificate issued by the market town of Wörgl : it softens sufferings dread; it offers work and bread."

Worgl Success

Over the 13-month period the Worgl money was in circulation, the mayor carried out all the intended works projects. The council also built new houses, a reservoir, a ski jump, and a bridge. The people also used scrip to replant forests, in anticipation of the future cash flow they would receive from the trees.

Six neighboring villages copied the system successfully. The French Prime Minister, Eduoard Dalladier, made a special visit to see the 'miracle of Wörgl'. In January 1933, the project was replicated in the neighboring city of Kirchbuhl, and in June 1933, Unterguggenburger addressed a meeting with representatives from 170 different towns and villages. Two hundred Austrian townships were interested in adopting the idea.

One eyewitness report was written by Claude Bourdet, master engineer from the Zürich Polytechnic. "I visited Wörgl in August 1933, exactly one year after the launch of the experiment. One has to acknowledge that the result borders on the miraculous. The roads, notorious for their dreadful state, match now the Italian Autostrade. The Mayor's office complex has been beautifully restored as a charming chalet with blossoming gladioli. A new concrete bridge carries the proud plaque: "Built with Free Money in the year 1933." Everywhere one sees new streetlights, as well as one street named after Silvio Gesell. The workers at the many building sites are all zealous supporters of the Free Money system. I was in the stores: the Bills are being accepted everywhere alongside with the official money. Prices have not gone up. Some people maintained that the system being experimented in Wörgl prevents the formation of equity, acting as a hidden new way of exploiting the taxpayer. There seems to be a little error in that view. Never before one saw taxpayers not protesting at the top of their voices when parting with their money. In Wörgl no one was protesting. On the contrary, taxes are paid in advance; people are enthusiastic about the experiment and complain bitterly at the National Bank's opposing the issuing of new notes. It is impossible to dub it only a "new form of tax" for the general improvement of Wörgl. One cannot but agree with the Mayor that the new money performs its function far better than the old one. I leave it to the experts to establish if there is inflation despite the 100% cover. Incidentally price increases, the first sign of inflation, do not occur. As far as saving is concerned one can say that the new money favors saving properly so-called rather than hoarding money. As money lost value by keeping it at home, one could avoid the depreciation by depositing in the savings bank.

Wörgl has become a kind of pilgrim shrine for macro-economists from a variety of countries. One can recognize them right away by their learned expressions when discussing the beautifully maintained streets of Wörgl while sitting at restaurant tables. Wörgl's population, proud of their fame, welcomes them warmly."

The Central Bank

The Central Bank panicked, and decided to assert its monopoly rights by banning complimentary currencies. The case was brought in front of the Austrian Supreme Court, which upheld the Central Banks monopoly over issuing currency. It then became a criminal offence to issue "emergency currency". Worgl quickly returned to 30% unemployment. Social unrest spread rapidly across Austria. In 1938 Hitler annexed Austria and many people welcomed Hitler as their economic and political savior.

Germany was headed towards WWII and with the aftermath of the war much of what happened in pre war Germany just like what happened during the war was suppressed by the world. Germany was being rebuilt in the West's image. The Worgl experiment was relegated to history.

Chapter 8: The New Investment Paradigm

The New Investment Paradigm

Gone are the days of savings and investments; government bonds and blue chips; technical analysis and fundamentals. Inflation, radical events, corporate crime, planet changes, and globalization have forever changed the face of the idea of 'investment'. The environment is too dynamic even for the seasoned trader - you can make the safest investment, into an energy company such as Enron, only to find out there are billions of dollars missing. Don't be too naive to think these are isolated incidents - they are not isolated to particular industry groups or even particular countries. Corporate fraud is as much prevalent in Europe and Asia as in the states, as are radical events, inflation, and freak weather. A bomb in London can cause financial chaos in markets across the board, as can a drought in Australia, freak storms in New Zealand, fires in California, or an earthquake in Tokyo. Welcome to the new paradigm of investment: interconnected global markets fueled by local catastrophes and lunatic leaders.

Traders and investment pros are now at the same level of the general public. Unless privy to insider information, they have no advanced skill that will enable them to make decisions in this dynamic environment. Their experience in the 'old system' is more of a hindrance than an advantage, because their mind is entrenched in the belief system that economics and fundamental analysis presides over geopolitical events and major catastrophic events, which leads to losses. While they continue to practice according to accepted standards, their loses can be justified, as no model can predict the kinds of events affecting the markets, and they will be left with no moral or legal liabilities. How can a trader investing in an Indian IT company expect that flooding will displace 2 million people from their homes?

Use the analogy of the 'help desk' - these are supposedly professionals you call when you don't know what to do - just like you invest in a fund not knowing where to put the money. Does the help desk actually give you information that you didn't know already? "Is your computer turned on, sir?" Or my favorite, "Sir, I'm sorry I don't have that number for tech support, but if you want to call them that's entirely up to you." Usually they are reading from the same web sites as you, and are not privy to special trade knowledge. Of course this is not always the case, some subjects are highly technical and also many people do not take the time to read-up on a subject, they want to make the call instead of spending the time to do it themselves, and that is the argument for a new group of traders vs. the general investing public. No longer is there a trade magic that you cannot do for yourself - however this doesn't mean you should do your own investing. If you are in any trade, you dedicate your time to that trade and not to watching the markets. No formal training or experience can prepare you for these market conditions - and those conditions will only multiply and get worse.

Radical events and the markets

Bank failures - Billions of dollars were made and lost on September 11, 2001. No investment, even keeping money in a bank, is safely protected by terrorist acts. Many panicked in the wake of the attack, trying to withdraw as much money as possible, to no avail. Now there are strict banking rules against withdrawing money - many accounts have a $2,000 per month limit. Larger amounts need to be 'ordered' weeks in advance - there simply isn't enough cash to go around.

Sinking USD - While Wall Street was closed for several days, currency traders and banks were selling USD like mad. Of course this was offset by US Fed interventions, still, we have a 40% decline in the dollar since then. Combined with inflation, the USD is even less valuable for consumers and investors purchasing US goods.

Crooks - Did anyone consider the amount of documents that were lost during the collapse of the WTC? We all saw the images of millions of pages of paper floating in the air, but no one seemed to think what was on that paper. The WTC was exactly that - a World Trade Center - of finance and trade. Posing that question to a few they all assumed there were backups of ALL documents lost in the disaster, not willing to believe in the Fight Club scenario where the credit records are destroyed and we all go back to zero. Yet in the confusion, a group of currency traders skated away with 100 million in client funds.

Earth Changes and the markets

Up until now, natural disasters have been long-term effects, because we still haven't seen 'the big one'. We see isolated events which only the extremely astute trader can pick up on. A major hurricane in Florida at the same time of a freak tornado storm in the Mid-West can bankrupt an insurance company who is exposed to both locations. This kind of stuff is what analysts in Wall Street get paid huge dollars to research; how the price of bananas in Brazil affects the share price of GE.

But what would happen to the property market of Florida for example, when news that global warming will rise the sea level by 100 feet hits the press? How about a Tsunami coming to London, a major financial district in the world marketplace. Yes it's a panic, but it's not the end of the world!

The pentagon is treating earth changes as a threat to national security. The way they see it, food and energy shortages will cause countries and individual groups to fight rather than starve. A country like India with nuclear capabilities may use their arsenal as a bargaining chip for trade deals involving basic food stock to feed their citizens. How will this affect the DOW, the CBOT, or the value of currencies?

Geo-political events and the markets

Bush signs the bill banning stem cell research. Dr. A from Germany calls Dr. B in Miami, "we have to shift the plant". Immediately they begin researching open free-market economies that will foster their type of research, and plan to move the plant. Within 6 months, they're gone, with their research and contributions to society. Along with hundreds of other genetic research companies now banned by the bush administration. These companies develop billion dollar products, it is not seen that they just dropped the US Dollar by billions of dollars, this is hidden, untraceable by the analysts.

Americans are getting slaughtered in Iraq. The battle is fierce and full of obstacles. Russians are supplying insurgents with GPS guided missiles and night vision equipment. Protestors form the largest protests ever seen, for any cause, ever: Dollar down. Wait a minute, now they've caught a tank. They've blown it up! It's on fire! Look on CNN! BBC! A tank on fire! Think of all those lucrative contracts American Corporates' will get! Buy Dollars!

Look at the value of the USD during the toppling of the Saddam statue. In the minds of people everywhere, that event signaled the end of the war, victory, and a new age of American hegemony in the middle east. Why? How did that statue change our military strategy, position our troops better? Information war, and that was a victory for propaganda in the minds of traders.

Inflation

It is hitting the economy at all fronts, some less obvious than others. Hidden Inflation is defined as: Price increased introduced by offering a smaller quantity or poorer quality at the same old price, hopefully you can notice this in the quality of everyday products you may use frequently. Going back to the basics, the old wives tales, old men sitting on the porch talking about 'they just don't make 'em like they used to'. That old man was talking about 'the good ole days' in the 20's or 30's, before many products such as clothing were handmade.

103

When I say it, I'm talking about the good ole days of 1999, before the bubble, when the USD Index was 120, when US foreign investment was running 40 billion a month, when I traveled to Europe and was greeted with warm smiles and curiosity (except the French who served me coke every time I ordered wine).

The Rumormill

There is a rally on Wall Street - rumor says they caught Bin Laden: nope, just another rumor. Larry Ellison died - Oracle plummets: nope, another rumor. Alan Greenspan had a heart attack! Oh shit he's just fine.

Who starts these rumors? How do they spread? What's the origin? Are these reflections of our gossiping society, or have we decided that rumors are more important than fundamentals? Do we all hope to get in on the action before it happens, and disinformation junkies are playing off our egos? Or is there no more real news and information, and traders rely on rumors simply because there is nothing left. We are all investing in hopes and dreams, like the great one that Yahoo is going to make a trillion dollars in 20 years.

Corporate Crime

All people are losing confidence in the corporate system. However, they are not given any choices. In the investment world for example, people look at large institutions as 'safe' and individuals with ideas 'crooks' - so now what is left for credibility? Stuffing your money under your mattress, or leaving it in a checking account gaining .25% interest, meanwhile the USD is down 30% and inflation is another 30% (that's in one year, now) and you're fucked. You don't know you're fucked, but soon enough you feel the pain. Talk about a transfer of wealth!

This is not a moral issue, like those evil capitalists in their corporate ivory towers flying in private gulfstream's while the investors are left holding the bag. It is an inquisition into these institutions themselves, how they are structured, how they came into existence historically, and now how they are being mechanically taken apart. Don't forget the idea from the beginning is to have these corporate sharks working for YOU, the shareholder. But they have grown stupid, lazy, decadent, non-sharkish, like little lambs playing with their lawyers and yachts. The golden parachute has no meaning. Gordon Gecko is dead.

Kozlowski threw a party in Sardinia, Italy featuring an ice sculpture of Michelangelo's David spewing vodka from his penis; for a total cost of $2M USD, including a $250,000 plane ticket for singer

Jimmy Buffett. Whether he used 'company money' or his money from his giant salary, what's the difference? Did anyone consider that this type of behavior is psychotic? How do you think Jane Investor felt who saved for 35 years working in a factory for minimum wage, and put her retirement (401k) into a company that she thought made little cute toys that she buys for her grand-daughters, only to find out her investment went into an exotic orgy in Italy, and to find the CEO charged with larceny? So much for cute fluffy toys, and bye-bye cute fluffy economy (you remember, how everything was about to be 'the next great thing'?). Will that image taint Jane Investors dreamy images of those fuzzy little creatures, stopping her from spending half of her pension buying them? Maybe she will knit them sweaters as presents instead. What Dennis did is he put Jane in a situation where she doesn't know what to buy her grandchildren as presents, and she doesn't know what to invest in.

Alternative Investments

If you have $50,000 to invest, you might consider buying some blue chip stocks at first. It would never occur to you to walk down the street and find a business financially strapped, become a silent capital partner, and get dividends Wall Street can only dream of. Small businesses have been beaten up by the nationalized corporate monopoly system, and are on the verge of extinction (See Wal-Mart destroys economies). Small town America is being taken over by companies like Wal-Mart, where now at their superstore; you can buy everything from health insurance to gasoline to milk. Everyone blames those evil corporate henchmen in their gulf streams, but really the fault lies with YOU, the small time investor. Instead of sending your money to New York, you could have been investing in these businesses that are being eaten up by giant multi-nationals like Wal-Mart and Microsoft.

Forex

During chaotic times, where to put the money, how to profit, how to protect wealth? How will Coca-Cola sell coke to countries whose infrastructure is destroyed or to Californians in the dark with no power grid? How can Google dominate the internet market when 95% of their customers are without power? Who will be the center of business during these kinds of times? How will other countries react to certain situations? Where will money flow and if certain systems fail how will businesses conduct their business (means of trade)? What kinds of businesses will be able to adapt to this dynamic environment? What start-ups will emerge in the aftermath, and what will not survive?

These are all questions that should be on a trader's mind.

105

Believers don't last very long in the currency market. An overall solution to this situation is to trade forex, the world's most liquid market. Wall Street can be shut down as can any major market exchange, but currencies need to flow one way or another. From any angle, if money stops flowing the world economy stops flowing, meaning stopping like instantly, back to the Stone Age. And as long as the money is flowing traders can ride the waves and protect their wealth. After 9/11 how long did it take Saudi's to transfer their funds out of the US? When you see the article 'Saudi Royalty transfers 100billion out of USA' do you think they just pick up the phone "Hey, George, I need another 100 billion" - they have hundreds of accounts, the funds are locked in CD's and term deposits and other investments, funds have to be cleared by the government on that level, they need a clearing bank, they have to fly over and physically sign documents, and find a place to put it after it leaves! What a nightmare!

NOT trading forex is losing. When you are invested in the DOW, in a bank deposit, in property, you are losing more and more exponentially. As business becomes more desperate (see Wal-Mart accidentally charging 80,000 credit cards), fees and taxes will increase, sharks and crooks will become more prevalent, crime will rise, insurance companies and other safe havens will not be able to back all claims, and the downward spiral continues.

Quasi Manipulation

Major market makers will attempt to manipulate the markets in their favor by staging events which will have effect on the markets. This is not a new concept, but the face of that method is changing. The initiators may be aware of this or not, it is the same result - a political event may carry the same weight as an economic report. These are the waves traders will ride to profit. Central Banks and governments play a large role, as they all want their currency to be cheaper. Countries are now competing with each other, who can inflate their currency more, making it less valuable, in order to obtain the more valuable foreign one.

A forex trader cannot live inside the system and hope to put a decision on all the events happening at once, as described here. You really need to think outside of the box, and live in a world conducive to that.

Boutique brokerage VS. Banks, Brokerage Houses

Traditionally there are certain social norms regarding money. You put cash in the bank, you invest in Wall Street, and buy children government savings bonds. As the institutions which reinforce these behaviors breakdown by fraud, losses, losers, and unethical business practices, people will more and more question those norms.

When you have cash, you are investing in Federal Reserve Notes. You are investing in the US Dollar, in Alan Greenspan, and in George Bush. You are assuming the currency will remain stable, inflation will be kept low, and there will not be too much of those FRN's floating around, making yours less and less valuable. Cash is becoming more and more a risky investment.

Before giving your money away to large institutions, an investor should understand how they work. These are large companies with huge overheads, and they operate in the realm of corporate feudalism. A client is just a number, a name on a screen, a tool for these organizations to perpetuate like a virus needs a host. They profit and the clients lose, in the long run. Sure you make a profit here and there, while clients don't even realize that after administration fees, taxes that could have easily been avoided, and corporate overhead, they are barely keeping up with inflation. Before John Q. Trader even thinks about clicking a button for you, he needs to:

Obtain a university degree such as an MBA from high-profile school like Wharton, costing him the 5 or 6 most productive *trading* years of his life, and $250,000. Get hired by that firm, be trained, buy a house, drive to work, put on a suit and tie, setup the office, buy an office plant, setup the computers and office infrastructure, and then start 'trading'. The firm needs to pay lawyers, marketing, other overheads, executives, accountants, fringe benefits, and finally, return profits to shareholders. How do the clients ever get any returns at all? The fact is these companies need the clients a lot more than the clients need the companies (to stay alive).

Imagine someone trading for themselves, because they see this as the only way out of this depression, just to stay ahead of the game. Trading $100,000 is the same like trading $100,000,000,000 - you are clicking the same buttons. Boutique Brokerages do not charge management fees, have no overhead, and invest their money before yours. If clients lose money, they lose money, and lose their lifestyle, maybe even their family. While it may sound like a leap forward in the investment business, would a client feel better about that, or a trader who makes $250,000 per year plus bonuses, regardless whether or not he makes money for the clients?

Now the problem: If you are a successful forex trader, and you obtain all the money you need - where do you invest?

In the new investment paradigm investors take care of their own positions. Large multi-national corporate investment houses are slow to adapt to a dynamic investment market, and losses are blamed on 'circumstances'. It is a transfer of wealth modern history has never seen, as we have not seen the power of computers and internet in the global money market.

Currently investment bankers, brokerage houses, and the entire corporate financial establishment, is desperately fighting for their survival. FIGHT FOR YOURS.

Chapter 9: FX Articles

EES US Investment Outlook Summer 2007

Recently financial markets have experienced more volatility than any historical period (since such volatility is being measured), according to a volatility index traded as a futures contract on the CME called the VIX. Aside from the anomalous trader profiting from the chaos, many investors have suffered large losses , and more importantly they are seeking safety in bonds and other debt-based instruments which have proven to be unsafe. Many previously high rated AAA bonds have been reduced to junk, and their exposure is almost everywhere. Many funds will invest in these risky bonds, either in the form of the repackaged sub-prime asset backed securities, or in the commercial paper market. For example, many money market funds had invested in CDO's, against the doctrine of the founder of money market funds, Bruce Bent.

"The money market fund was created to provide effective cash management, to guarantee at least a dollar in and a dollar back and beyond that, a reasonable rate of return," Mr Bent says.

Driven by fear, investors have moved quickly into treasuries, a 'flight to safety'.

Aug. 20 (Bloomberg) -- Yields on U.S. Treasury bills fell the most in two decades on demand for the safest securities amid concern over a widening credit crunch.

Bill yields have fallen five straight days as money market funds dumped asset-backed commercial paper in favor of the shortest-maturity government debt. Three-month yields dropped the most since the stock market crash of 1987 and more than in the wake of the Sept. 11, 2001, terror attacks in the U.S, as funds shunned assets that may be linked to a weakening mortgage market.

``The market is totally, absolutely, completely in fear mode," said John Jansen, who sells Treasuries at CastleOak Securities LP in New York. ``People are afraid that lots and lots of mortgage paper and mortgage paper derivatives of all sorts is completely opaque and they can't price it."

The three-month Treasury bill yield fell 0.66 percentage point to 3.09

percent as of 5:06 p.m. in New York. It's the most since Oct. 20,
1987, when the yield fell 85 basis points on the day the stock market
crashed, and eclipses the drop of 39 basis points on Sept. 13, 2001,
the day the Treasury market reopened after the attacks. The yield has
fallen from 4.69 percent on Aug. 13. The bills yielded about 7 percent
in mid-October 1987 and 3.2 percent in the days before the
September 2001 attacks.

``I've never seen it like this before," said Jim Galluzzo, who began
trading short-maturity Treasuries 20 years ago and now trades bills at
RBS Greenwich Capital in Greenwich, Connecticut. ``Bills right now
are trading like dot-coms."

However, treasuries are still US Dollar based. If Bernake lowers rates,
and continues to lower, as indicated by the sentiment of traders, it can
only sink the already sinking dollar more. In the next 12 months, if the
dollar drops another 20%, and your treasuries have yielded 5%, your
net gain is negative 15%. This may seem like simple arithmetic, yet no
analyst on the street is mentioning the currency trade. They all know
the carry trade, and that it's unwinding, but this is looked at as
speculative trading activity. No one is commenting on the greater
economic and investment impact of the 'credit crunch' as it relates to
the dollar, and what it means for US based investors. They see the
problem but not the solution. The current credit crisis is simple to
understand.

- Average weekly wage as of December 2006 is $861 ($44,772 annually)

- Number of employed persons in US nationally is 135,933,200

- Total earnings is 5.7 trillion, GDP is 13.1 trillion (7.3 trillion sur-minus)

- Total national debt is 9 trillion

- Trade deficit is -$763.6 billion in 2006

The US doesn't have a surplus; we have a *sur-minus*. This is known as
the national debt, but it comes in many forms. One claim is that we
have a double deficit, that is, a current account deficit and a fiscal
deficit. The consumer, the US government, and US based corporations
all have negative savings rates, meaning they spend more money than
they have.

110

What enables the economy to function in the red is a simple credit mechanism, which is unfortunately not backed by anything other than belief in USA. At some point, as the case with the credit market, there could be a 'tipping point' that could cause a whirlwind of dollar selling, a 'flight to convertibles' similar to the credit 'flight to safety'. Even the IMF states in a report that the USD is 30% overvalued.

Many stock analysts are recommending companies based on their overseas operations, placing a great value on companies that derive a great portion of their revenue from offshore markets. This is not a vote of confidence in sophisticated multinational operations; it is a derivative dollar short. These corporations are profiting in Euros and Pounds, and therefore have more gross revenue when repatriating those profits back home in the US Dollar, inflating their revenue by the value of the dollar decline. An investor doesn't need to invest in these stocks in order to profit by a dollar decline; one may simply short the dollar.

Shorting the dollar if you are a US based investor is a natural hedge, because if your trade is wrong, you will benefit from a long dollar position in your savings account (which is dollar based). It seems like a no-brainer, why isn't everyone doing it?

Real estate no longer is an appealing investment (if it ever was). Stocks are currently suffering due to subprime 'credit crisis' related exposure. Bonds are being downgraded to junk; ratings agencies rank bonds AAA one day and junk when they collapse, so what is the point of purchasing high-rated debt instruments?

EES proposes the following:

- Structured foreign exchange products offered to retail investors. Forex Managed Accounts with a track record, packaged as a structured forex investment.

- "Dollar short" automated strategies, that pick points to short the dollar based on momentum based indicators and RSI "overbought" style indicators. Instead of taking 1 simple dollar short position, an automated system could day-trade a falling dollar, locking in short term profits and hedge against losing trades.

- Principle protected products in a risky forex strategy, where only a % of cash is traded with high leverage. For example using a 1m fund, 100k is invested into high risk forex strategies, protecting 90% of capital 100%.

**For more detail please visit Elite E Services at:
www.eliteeservices.net**

State of current Automated Trading

The current state of automation is human designed, rule based trading. That means, a professional trader can think about what rules he wants to implement, code them, test, and execute. This is, no doubt, a powerful tool for traders.

When trading at Refco, we noticed a discrepancy that the EUR/USD would move 20 – 50 points up every Sunday, but only at Refco. Like clockwork, we took it for 10 – 20 points every Sunday. This went on for months. That strategy could be easily codified, and so long as the market continues to perform that way, it would have profited. But eventually, Refco collapsed, and the company no longer is trading. So now, the strategy would be worthless, automated or not.

It is very tricky business to establish patterns in charts and technical indicators based on market cycles, because there are always instances in these patterns thrown off by various human – based factors such as news, national holidays, events, weather, etc.

Rule based trading is a powerful addition to a trader's toolbox – but is by no means the holy grail. Our rule-based trading systems are static. They can be optimized and updated, but they cannot self-adjust. That means we need to regularly monitor them, and sometimes make changes. What we propose to create with the FATS project is a strategy that self-adjusts to market conditions in real time, something which does not exist.

The current strategies we have, may or may not work depending on the skill of the trader. So they are fully automated in the sense that you can walk away from the computer, and they will not require any intervention. However, they need to be constantly tweaked, adjusted, and optimized.

- Common sense cannot be codified: If the EUR/USD goes up 40% many bullish buy-side strategies may trigger buys, but common sense will tell you it's risky to buy at such high levels. While this can be codified in a filter, if that has never happened before, systems traders may not have seen a reason to codify such a filter

- The world changes: The market adjusts to new players, such as China floating the Yuan, central banks pumping liquidity into the markets, and so on. Therefore, only a dynamic strategy can consistently profit

There is no dynamic self-adjusting strategy on the market. What we are using now, are off the shelf commercial software products such as Meta Trader, which offer the ability to code your strategy based on certain parameters. Meta Trader is nothing more than an opportunity for humans to create rule-based strategies, whereas the FATS engine will implement an Artificial Intelligence strategy creation engine, that tells Meta Trader where to trade.

What is automatic now, is the execution, what we want to make automatic, is the strategy creation.

Forex Market Education

Is it ironic that the currency market, driver of global trade and finance, without a doubt the most significant market in the world economy and politics, is the least known? Why is there such a void of information, and why are there so many misnomers regarding currency trading and investing?

From a traders perspective, the forex market is easier to trade in terms of execution and reporting, market hours (forex is 24/7), leverage (400:1), and ability to implement technical systems. There are only 8 major currency pairs, which have limited range, and are correlated mathematically.

In the stock market, the largest concern is insider trading. Insider trading is illegal in the stock market, because it is a specific unfair advantage that corporate officers have due to sensitive information they have. However, insider trading is not illegal in the currency market, because there are no 'insiders', and also it is not unethical for a bank to sell currency because that is the business of the bank! Insider trading does not apply to the currency market; in fact it is the least regulated market in the world – because it is a money market. Currency traders are trading money for money, the highest form of trading. Every currency trade is determining the value of money.

At the bottom of the economic chain you have people who trade their manual labor for money. Then you have people who trade their goods for money, such as seen in futures and commodities markets. Finally you have those who trade pure information for money, which is information brokerage and some forms of Information Technology. Finally you have people who trade money for money, which is banking. Since we have abandoned the Breton Woods treaty and have a free floating currency exchange system, now another layer of complexity has been added, which is money being valued in terms of other money.

The reason for mentioning this is to illustrate that currency markets affect everyone. When the dollar is going down, it is decreasing in its purchasing power, creating inflation. This is not a commonly known mechanism because although the abandonment of Breton woods has completely changed our worldwide financial system, new books have not been written according to the new rules of the game. People think inflation comes naturally from the business cycle, when in fact it comes from the printing of money which creates oversupply. Now, with the new paradigm of money creation connected to forex trading, another element exists in the inflation equation that didn't exist before. Foreigners can buy your local currency and dry up supply. This motivates local central banks to print more currency to compensate and, thus we have a new inflationary paradigm of currencies each competing for their own destruction – the game is who can inflate more, quicker.

Especially in a world of globalization heavily dependent on global trade, specifically in the G8 and industrialized nations, the value of a countries currency exactly determines how many goods and services can be purchased and imported. Of course, if we can use our financial monopoly to decimate their currency and have more products for ourselves, all the better. International trade can take place by exchanging goods for goods – a sophisticated form of bartering. Or, we can manufacture money and purchase overseas goods backed by our banking system, which everyone is happy to accept so they can go out and purchase other goods from other countries (and a small % from us as well).

This delicate balance of financial power is demonstrated in the currency market, because of the mechanical procedure involved in remitting funds overseas. You need to exchange your dollars for Euros, and when you do so you pay the price. Banks take no risk in the game and act as accountants for funds going back and forth from one currency to another.

Maybe a reason that there is little knowledge about forex is because the focus has always been on the mechanical aspect and not the economic impact. Maybe the financial establishment does not want to mention the fact that the reason the DOW is 13,000 is because the dollar is down, and a weak dollar is fuelling a real estate boom, and that real estate is just a gauge of inflation. Or maybe few understand the new paradigm of foreign exchange and the real value of money. Either way, there is little public information and understanding on the topic which is more significant than any other in modern finance.

Having said all of the above, you may wonder how to invest in such a market. There are basically 2 sides to the forex market; hedgers and speculators. Hedgers include any business or individual that is trading currency out of need – you sell your products overseas and require foreign currency or have multiple currencies budgeting in international markets. The second group (which is by far the minority) is speculators such as hedge funds and investment banks who take positions in the currency market with the hope for financial profit. The mechanism the speculators use to profit varies widely – from long term investment in a currency, to trading an automated 'day trading' system which takes many small trades in a day. There are also many strategies traders use that can become quite complex due to the mathematical relationship between currencies. For example there is triangular relationship between any 3 cross-pairs (for example EUR/USD, EUR/CHF, and USD/CHF). A trader may develop a strategy to capitalize on that relationship, or use it to 'hedge out' of a position by reducing his net exposure without taking on new positions. This type of strategy is unique to the forex market because of the cross pair system and the relationship between them. Other markets require derivatives to create such strategies (such as equity futures and options).

When investing in the currency market, one can find a professional trader who knows what he is doing, and evaluate the performance of different strategies and select one which matches his investment goals and risk profile. Some strategies are more risky than others, and there is a correlation between risk and reward. Many so called 'hedging systems' can work for months gaining as much as 50% per month, but always risk wiping out the account completely. Then there are more conservative strategies that may return 2% to 5% per month, less exciting but much less risky. Of course every strategy involves risk, there is no such strategy that is risk free in trading, and that is why no fund or trader can offer a guaranteed return. It is impossible to forecast a large amount of variables that could lead to losses.

No one is suggesting you shift your entire portfolio into fx - but a little education about the largest and most liquid market in the world, certainly wouldn't hurt any investor.

www.fxcyberschool.com

- Joe Gelet, CTA www.eliteeservices.net

Forex Automated Brokerage

The financial establishment, defined as large banks, brokerage houses, and multinational financial corporations such as Goldman Sachs, JP Morgan Chase, Citigroup, Deutsche Bank, etc., think that speculating in FX is a useless activity because 'there is no money in spot forex'. They trade bonds, stocks, futures, options, and newly formed exotic derivatives such as Swaptions (Options on interest rate swaps). In their view, you cannot make money by trading money itself, and foreign exchange is not a speculator's market like the Stock market is. These companies control trillions in client capital, and they have very few, if any, clients trading in managed forex products. The traditional financial establishment considers forex to be something not worth investing in or developing strategies for. Why they have this view is another discussion, here we are simply describing the current forex business environment worldwide and stating facts as we know. Velocity 4x, FXCM, Gain Capital, GFT Forex, Interbank FX, and others, are rogue companies founded by various kinds of people, sometimes FX traders who came from desks at reputable established firms such as Credit Suisse. FXCM was founded with $500,000 in 1999 and in 2007 they will likely see over $1 billion in revenue. The brokers have been exploding in all measurable ways, and this is going on quietly without the consent of the real players in financial world, the big names. Yet, FXCM was spending 4 million a month just in Google ads! www.cnn.com is flooded with FXCM ads. They open 4,000 new accounts per month. Since Forex is unregulated, and because there are no rules as to how you need to trade or clear forex trades, the costs of opening a forex brokerage are 1% to 2% that of a traditional brokerage, such as a Stock Brokerage. In fact, a forex brokerage is now comprised of a series of servers, and support staff. Each broker in current operation has taken a very distinctive and different view as to how to run a brokerage. A Russian company "MetaQuotes" offers a boxed solution to purchase their product "MetaTrader" for $150,000 which can manage the entire order flow of the clients and back office as well. Meta Trader offers "Expert Advisor" trading systems which are automatically executed forex trading strategies. Clients using MetaTrader are free to develop and trade their own strategy. The advantage of MetaTrader is that it is a standard of auto trading so a client can take his strategy to another broker and trade it. The huge disadvantage is that the software itself has many inconsistencies, and you always rely on the MetaTrader package although they do not make public any technical documentation. It is fair enough that Microsoft does not open its code to the public, but when a trade goes against you and you lose $25,000 you have no way to explain it (because the strategy does not do what you program it to). The problem is that you are limited to the confines of MetaTrader, which is by no means a bad software package. It is however limited in its features and also there are liquidity issues with many brokers that are unresolved. There are a growing number of traders who have automated systems that brokers cannot provide enough liquidity for. That means their infrastructure cannot handle their strategy. They have the money and are ready to trade, if we can offer them more sophisticated software solutions for the clearing and execution of their trading strategies. It is our proposal to fill this need. We understand the need because we

116

are traders and programmers, we do not come from brokerage industry. It is also for this reason why we can implement this concept and the brokers cannot. They feel they are doing more than enough for clients like us, although there is a large gap they cannot fill. Aside from traditional business infrastructure (offices) we would require a specialized programming team and computer hardware in order to create this company. Out of the box servers would not be appropriate for example. We should design custom servers using CELL processor technology, combined with a cluster of Blade Servers running various tasks such as strategy execution and risk management. It would take us 18 months to finish the complete model, but if we develop in stages we could begin making money after 8 months. That means we will develop module by module, finally finishing with complete money management brokerage software that is completely integrated from the client side to the back office and administration. *Liquidity:* Our liquidity can be sourced in several ways but it is not a large issue. Various brokers offer API connections which we can plug into our clearing module. That means we can actually clear our trades with other brokers! In this sense we would be creating a global forex ECN (Electronic Communications Network) that would be a new kind of forex market. As new brokers offer liquidity, we can add them to the list of providers. In this way, we can maximize our liquidity potential and minimize our capital risk and technical risk in the event any single provider goes down. Some of the providers may be banks, Currenex, or other ECN's such as Hotspot or EBS. The multi-provider approach is in our view, the only appropriate solution for sourcing FX liquidity. *How to find clients?* Clients will find us. Our concept will be unique and the automated trading community is a small one. Word will spread quickly that there is a 'techie broker' who is actually doing things properly. We should be totally private, not have a public website, and have a $100,000 minimum. EES has existing clients who would open accounts in this brokerage immediately. *Weakness of traditional brokerage:* For many clients, traditional brokers are working very well. This project is not about picking apart the fallacies of the bricks and mortar brokerages that exist. Rather, we are pointing out what these brokerages lack, most significantly, they cannot cater to a number of automated traders who have a lot of trading capital to invest. *Risk Factors:* As we are developing a business out of a need displayed by traders and programmers, the risks of this project are very low. We know what customers need and are providing them a service at a fair commission sharing revenue model. We always run the risk of some major market shifts such as the world abandoning the floating FX system, where currencies are pegged to each other. In that case we imagine we could use our system on other markets. *Our Client Advantage:* The niche of system traders is the most profitable in the business. Because they have calculated systems that usually

117

create large volume. 90% of the profit and trade volume is created by 10% of trading accounts. Our brokerage is targeting those 10% of active accounts, so we will have fewer clients in numbers but those few clients will generate 10x the volume than normal clients. *Revenue* See this below account statement as a reference for revenue and our client model.

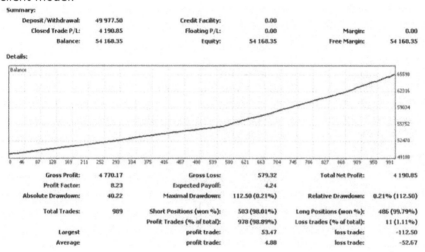

This system generated in 2 days, $11,595.00 in commissions for the broker and $4,190.85 in profit for the client. This client alone could generate $3,061,080 million in profit per year for us, assuming 264 days in a trading year. That is of course assuming the account remained at the same level of activity, and it is very safe to assume that as the client is profitable he would deposit more funds and the activity would increase. If we could find 10 such clients, our revenue for the year would be $30 million our first year. If this account was funded with $500,000 instead of $50,000 you can add a zero. So only 10 clients trading in this fashion would generate $300 million in revenue for the firm without doing any marketing, and we know more than 10 people who have this interest, money, and capability.

Chapter 10: Forex, Version 1 – A managed accounts program

What would any explanation of forex be without a real example to reference?

A forex managed accounts program which is 100% systematic, based on actual live performance of automated systems trading in real time.

Each strategy has a track record proving it's performance before trading client money. Strategies represent the top 1% of a pool of thousands of forex strategies, qualified to trade your account. The portfolio approach ensures that if one strategy loses, another will compensate for the losses, giving an overall result which is consistent, steady, robust, positive. Target returns are 10% - 20% per month, with no more than 5% drawdown.

Risk Disclosure Documents& Managed Account Agreement

FXV1
Forex, Version 1
100% Systematic Foreign Exchange Trading Managed Accounts Program

NOTICE: This disclosure document has been reprinted in this publication for the purposes of educating the reader as to the technicalities of investing in foreign exchange. It could be updated, for the latest version please visit www.fxv1.com This document should not be treated as an account application or full disclosure document. For the full document please contact Elite E Services at www.eliteeservices.net or visit www.fxv1.com

THE COMMODITY FUTURES TRADING COMMISSION HAS NOT PASSED UPON THE MERITS OF PARTICIPATING IN THIS TRADING PROGRAM NOR HAS THE COMMISSION PASSED ON THE ADEQUACY OR ACCURACY OF THIS DISCLOSURE DOCUMENT.

Wednesday, August 1st, 2007

The delivery of this Disclosure Brochure does not at any time imply that the information contained herein is correct as of any time subsequent to the date shown above. This Disclosure Brochure may not be used or distributed under any circumstances after November 1, 2007 and will be superseded on that date by a Disclosure Brochure containing then current information about this Trading Strategy. Information herein is from sources believed to be reliable, but its accuracy cannot be guaranteed. Readers using this information are solely responsible for their actions and invest at their own risk. No part of this publication may be reproduced or re-transmitted without specific written consent from the editor. Trademarks and other copyrights are of Elite E Services, Incorporated. Any and all unauthorized reproduction is strictly prohibited.

RISK DISCLOSURE STATEMENT

THE RISK OF LOSS IN TRADING COMMODITIES CAN BE SUBSTANTIAL. YOU SHOULD THEREFORE CAREFULLY CONSIDER WHETHER SUCH TRADING IS SUITABLE FOR YOU IN LIGHT OF YOUR FINANCIAL CONDITION. IN CONSIDERING WHETHER TO TRADE OR TO AUTHORIZE SOMEONE ELSE TO TRADE FOR YOU, YOU SHOULD BE AWARE OF THE FOLLOWING: IF YOU PURCHASE A COMMODITY OPTION, YOU MAY SUSTAIN A TOTAL LOSS OF THE PREMIUM AND OF ALL TRANSACTION COSTS. IF YOU PURCHASE OR SELL A COMMODITY FUTURE OR SELL A COMMODITY OPTION, YOU MAY SUSTAIN A TOTAL LOSS OF THE INITIAL MARGIN FUNDS AND ANY ADDITIONAL FUNDS THAT YOU DEPOSIT WITH YOUR BROKER TO ESTABLISH OR MAINTAIN YOUR POSITION. IF THE MARKET MOVES AGAINST YOUR POSITION, YOU MAY BE CALLED UPON BY YOUR BROKER TO DEPOSIT A SUBSTANTIAL AMOUNT OF ADDITIONAL MARGIN FUNDS, ON SHORT NOTICE, IN ORDER TO MAINTAIN YOUR POSITION. IF YOU DO NOT PROVIDE THE REQUESTED FUNDS WITHIN THE PRESCRIBED TIME, YOUR POSITION MAY BE LIQUIDATED AT A LOSS, AND YOU WILL BE LIABLE FOR ANY RESULTING DEFICIT IN YOUR ACCOUNT. UNDER CERTAIN MARKET CONDITIONS, YOU MAY FIND IT DIFFICULT OR IMPOSSIBLE TO LIQUIDATE A POSITION. THIS CAN OCCUR, FOR EXAMPLE, WHEN THE MARKET MAKES A "LIMIT MOVE." THE PLACEMENT OF CONTINGENT ORDERS BY YOU OR YOUR TRADING ADVISOR, SUCH AS A "STOP-LOSS" OR "STOP-LIMIT" ORDER, WILL NOT NECESSARILY LIMIT YOUR LOSSES TO THE INTENDED AMOUNTS, SINCE MARKET CONDITIONS MAY MAKE IT IMPOSSIBLE TO EXECUTE SUCH ORDERS. A "SPREAD" POSITION MAY NOT BE LESS RISKY THAN A SIMPLE "LONG" OR "SHORT" POSITION. THE HIGH DEGREE OF LEVERAGE THAT IS OFTEN OBTAINABLE IN COMMODITY TRADING CAN WORK AGAINST YOU AS WELL AS FOR YOU.

THE USE OF LEVERAGE CAN LEAD TO LARGE LOSSES AS WELL AS GAINS.

IN SOME CASES, MANAGED COMMODITY ACCOUNTS ARE SUBJECT TO

SUBSTANTIAL CHARGES FOR MANAGEMENT AND ADVISORY FEES. IT MAY BE NECESSARY FOR THOSE ACCOUNTS THAT ARE SUBJECT TO THESE CHARGES TO MAKE SUBSTANTIAL TRADING PROFITS TO AVOID DEPLETION OR EXHAUSTION OF THEIR ASSETS. THIS DISCLOSURE DOCUMENT CONTAINS, AT PAGE 15, A COMPLETE DESCRIPTION OF EACH FEE TO BE CHARGED TO YOUR ACCOUNT BY THE COMMODITY TRADING ADVISOR. THIS BRIEF STATEMENT CANNOT DISCLOSE ALL THE RISKS AND OTHER SIGNIFICANT ASPECTS OF THE COMMODITY MARKETS. YOU SHOULD THEREFORE CAREFULLY STUDY THIS DISCLOSURE DOCUMENT AND COMMODITY TRADING BEFORE YOU TRADE, INCLUDING THE DESCRIPTION OF THE PRINCIPAL RISK FACTORS OF THIS INVESTMENT, AT PAGE 18.   YOU SHOULD ALSO BE AWARE THAT THIS COMMODITY TRADING ADVISOR MAY ENGAGE IN TRADING FOREIGN FUTURES OR OPTIONS CONTRACTS. TRANSACTIONS ON MARKETS LOCATED OUTSIDE THE UNITED STATES, INCLUDING MARKETS FORMALLY LINKED TO A UNITED STATES MARKET MAY BE SUBJECT TO REGULATIONS WHICH OFFER DIFFERENT OR DIMINISHED PROTECTION. FURTHER, UNITED STATES REGULATORY AUTHORITIES MAY BE UNABLE TO COMPEL THE ENFORCEMENT OF THE RULES OF REGULATORY AUTHORITIES OR MARKETS IN NON-UNITED STATES JURISDICTIONS WHERE YOUR TRANSACTIONS MAY BE EFFECTED. BEFORE YOU TRADE YOU SHOULD INQUIRE ABOUT ANY RULES RELEVANT TO YOUR PARTICULAR CONTEMPLATED TRANSACTIONS AND ASK THE FIRM WITH WHICH YOU INTEND TO TRADE FOR DETAILS ABOUT THE TYPES OF REDRESS AVAILABLE IN BOTH YOUR LOCAL AND OTHER RELEVANT JURISDICTIONS.

Disclosure Statement:

THIS COMMODITY TRADING ADVISOR (CTA) IS PROHIBITED BY LAW FROM ACCEPTING FUNDS IN THE TRADING ADVISOR'S NAME FROM A CLIENT FOR TRADING COMMODITY INTERESTS. YOU MUST PLACE ALL FUNDS FOR TRADING IN THIS TRADING PROGRAM DIRECTLY WITH A FUTURES COMMISSION MERCHANT.

SPECIFIC FOREX RISK DISCLOSURE STATEMENT

BEFORE PROCEEDING, YOU MUST READ AND AGREE TO OR DECLINE THE FOLLOWING INVESTMENT DISCLAIMER

The risk of loss in trading foreign exchange markets (FOREX), also known as cash foreign currencies, the inter-bank market or the FOREX markets, can be substantial. You should therefore carefully consider whether such trading is suitable for you given your financial condition. Elite E Services, Inc. (EES) does not control, and cannot endorse or vouch for the accuracy or completeness of any information or advice you may have received or may receive in the future from any other person not employed by EES regarding foreign currency trading or any managed account information. The factual information contained herein has been obtained from sources believed to be reliable but is NOT necessarily all-inclusive and is NOT guaranteed to be 100% accurate. The content herein is provided on a best efforts basis and is believed to be up-to-date and accurate; however, there are no explicit or implicit warranties of accuracy or timeliness made by EES or affiliates. FOREX trading involves substantial risk and is not for all investors. Investments or trading in the FOREX markets can be highly speculative and should only be done with risk capital which you can afford to lose and that, if lost, would not change or adversely affect your lifestyle. The high degree of leverage that is often possible in foreign exchange trading can work for you as well as against you. The use of leverage can lead to large losses as well as gains. Managed foreign exchange accounts can be subject to substantial charges for management and profit incentive fees, and in some cases (Introducing Brokers, Referring Parties) commissions or mark-ups that are above and beyond the ordinary spread generally provided on a clearing firm's trade execution platform. It may be necessary for those accounts that are subject to these charges to make substantial trading profits to avoid depletion or exhaustion of their assets. Performance results may vary due to account size, starting or closing date, the number of positions and/or markets traded and/or other factors. The regulations of the Commodity Futures Trading Commission (CFTC) require that prospective customers of a Futures Commission Merchant (FCM) or Clearing House receive a disclosure document when they are solicited. These disclosures are incorporated into the Managed Account Agreement and the Limited Power of Attorney (LPOA) below. This brief statement cannot disclose all of the risks and other significant aspects of the foreign exchange markets. Therefore, you should carefully review the disclosures contained in this document to determine whether such trading is appropriate for you in light of you particular financial condition. There are also risks associated with utilizing an internet-based deal execution system software application, and computerized trading and money management tools including, but not limited to, the failure of the hardware and software.

PAST PERFORMANCE DOES NOT NECESSARILY GUARANTEE FUTURE RESULTS, nor does it guarantee freedom from losses. The information contained herein should not be construed as an offer to buy or sell commodities, futures, securities, or any type of investment. EES highly recommends that before making a decision, the reader collects several opinions related to the decision and verify facts from several independent sources.

Elite E Services Foreign Exchange Risk Disclosure

Trading foreign exchange is extremely risky. Even without the use of leverage, there is a chance that substantial losses may be incurred.

Any investor should only invest funds they feel comfortable losing. For example, a savings or retirement account would not be appropriate for forex investment.

About the market – why it is risky

Forex is a fast moving, complex market which can be subject to fluctuation by political event, unforeseen forces such as natural disasters, or even the weather. Even dynamic mathematical models of leading hedge funds can be thrown off by these factors, generating losses. There is no holy grail to trading, and every trading strategy has a flaw, given enough time. There is no infallible strategy which will work all the time, with perfection.

It is not recommended that you count on any returns in forex market. If a fund made 2% last month, there is no reason to expect 2% this month.

The forex market is for the professional, sophisticated investor. For more information please visit our website: **http://ees.net.nz/legal.htm**

EES will apply the trading systems and traders listed here, to the best of our ability. Although we take the greatest care in filtering our trades, and selecting and designing our systems, that does not mean they will work all the time, and we cannot guarantee anything.

By signing here, you agree that you understand the above risk disclosure statements. Elite E Services, or our forex broker, or any other involved parties cannot be held responsible for any losses, nor do we guarantee any results. Past performance is not an indication of future results.

_____

_____

Signature   **Leverage**

_____

Printed Name

_____

Date

Table of Contents

*Pages unnumbered – attached at end of document. This is actual account opening application, do not send entire disclosure document to FXCM.

Account opening can be done online via www.fxv1.com

For more information please visit our website at:

www.fxv1.com

Introduction

Elite E Services Incorporated (EES) is a registered Nevada corporation that develops foreign exchange trading systems and technology. EES is a registered CTA with the CFTC and an NFA Member. NFA ID: 0373609.

Program Name

FXV1 meaning 'Forex, Version 1'

Investment Type

Managed FX Account Program comprised of a portfolio of automatically generated strategies. Day trading systems traded regularly that are constantly in and out of the market, with the aim of taking multiple high-probability trades with minimum risk.

Account Type

A managed account is an investment account, in your name, where a Limited Power of Attorney is given to a professional money manager, in this case, Elite E Services and our trading partner Forex Bot Limited. Clients do not need to have an in-depth knowledge of the forex market, however it is recommended that you understand forex as explained in this document that you have understanding of the style of trading and the dynamics of foreign exchange.

The FOREX market

The international foreign-exchange market is also known as the cash foreign exchange market, the FOREX Market, the currency market, the inter-bank FX market, over-the-counter (OTC) currency market or simply FX. The FOREX market is a 24 hour global market that has been dominated by multinational banks, institutions and large corporations for decades. Corporations use the foreign exchange markets to hedge cash-flows, and assets & liabilities such as property and non-domestic accounts receivable/payables held/owed in various foreign currencies. FOREX is by far the largest and most liquid market in the world, with daily trading volume of approximately $1.5 to $3.0 trillion US dollars per day, compared with approximately only $30 billion USD per day on the New York Stock Exchange.

Opportunity

Trading in The FOREX market is the best means by which to capitalize on a country or region's perceived economic, political, financial or environmental strengths/weaknesses, or relative changes in interest rate differentials between countries. Moreover, currencies are known for maintaining strong trending characteristics in both up and down markets, through wars, periods of inflation and recessions. FOREX trading is also unique in that offers the possibility of greater leverage than is typical in other asset-classes, which can work both for or against you.

No Trading Restrictions

Also, unlike most stocks traded on US exchanges that require a price "up-tick" in order to sell short, in the FOREX market it's as easy to sell-short as it is to buy. The Forex market can also never reach pre-determined movement "limits" as exists in futures, or be "halted" as stocks sometimes are.

Lower Systemic Trading Costs

Unlike trading in futures, stocks, mutual funds, options or other asset-classes, Forex Trading generally involves low commissions (approx. $15/100k Round Turn), no clearing fees, no exchange fees or other transaction costs imposed by the clearing firm. And since bid/ask spreads can be exceptionally tight, the net transaction and execution cost of trading in the Forex market compares favorably to other markets. Another potential benefit is that there are virtually no price gaps with the exception of during a weekend because FOREX is traded 24 hrs per day, generally from Sunday 5:00 PM EST until Friday 5:00 PM EST . And due to its unparalleled liquidity, trade execution slippage tends to be less of an issue for large traders when compared to most other markets. For these reasons, many of the world's largest banks, money managers and traders trade in the FOREX markets. FXV1 aims to exploit these advantages as well.

The FXV1 program does involve per trade transaction fees, performance fees, and management fees. The above statement is meant to compare the overall transaction costs of trading forex vs. other markets, which makes it a more lucrative market for systems traders.

Principals and Managers

About Joe Gelet

Joe Gelet is the president and head trader of Elite E Services.

Joe Gelet is a creative entrepreneur who has a diverse experience set. He grew up in Boca Raton amidst an economic, social, and technological boom. Not only was Boca an interesting melting pot of cultures and business people, IBM research and development was there, and Boca is known as the birthplace of the PC. What South Florida is less known for is the connection to trading and the markets. South Florida is home to hundreds of small trading firms, Tradestation Securities, and home to many famous traders.

Joe attended Pine Crest Prep School in Ft. Lauderdale, FL since he was 3 years old. He left 2 years to start his trading career at the age of 16. After obtaining his GED, he studied the markets and attended several educational seminars on day-trading, a growing trend at the time. By 1998, Day-Trading was growing in popularity, as was the NASDAQ and the infamous .com stocks. It may have been unlucky timing for learning to trade but lucky for making money, as random trades long the NASDAQ would have likely resulted in short-term profits. However we all know how that story ended; in 2000 trading became more difficult, when Joe began researching and learning forex. Since then he has been trading and developing trading technologies and running Elite E Services, an electronic boutique brokerage he co-founded with 3 partners in New Zealand. In 2004 EES built a custom designed trading studio in South Carolina, where they develop and trade to this day.

Academic Institutions

- Northwood University (Banking and Finance) Joe attended NU from the years of 1999-2002 where he met his business partners who founded Elite E Services collectively

- Brigham Young University (Philosophy, Psychology, Economics) Correspondence Courses taken in the above subjects

- Institute for Financial Markets (Series 3 training) Last year Joe obtained his Series 3 license and is now a registered CTA with the NFA

Trading related skills

Joe has been actively managing accounts since 1997, giving him 10 years active trading experience.

- Designed and programmed Forex Signal generating systems

featured on popular trading websites "Intrepidus", a fearless counter-trending Bollinger system surprising critics trade by trade (made 19/20 successful trades on the hourly chart in 3 months)

- Traded for a boutique currency fund in New Zealand as one of the most successful traders, using technical analysis from Commerzbank as a guide, manually executed on the SaxoBank platform
- Has programmed trading systems and indicators in Meta Trader and Tradestation platforms
- Consultant to several FCM's for trading, programming and trading related I.T.
- As the President of Elite E Services, Joe has gained industry experience in starting and managing a financial services firm

There has never been any material administrative, civil or criminal actions (whether pending, on appeal or concluded) against Mr. Gelet. Mr. Gelet is registered with the NFA, **Joe Gelet's NFA ID:** 0364715. He is the principal of Elite E Services and holds the CTA for EES.

• ASSOCIATED PERSON REGISTERED

• PRINCIPAL APPROVED

Elite E Services (EES)

EES is a Nevada registered Corporation with registered offices at:

Elite E Services contact information

Website: www.eliteeservices.net

Email: info@eliteeservices.net

Skype: eliteeservices
Phone: 800- 975-8581

DDL NY: 646-837-0059

Corporate Address EES USA

Elite E. Services Inc.

2620 Regatta Dr. Suite 102

Las Vegas, NV 89128

Elite E Services Limited was established in New Zealand in September 2002, and still operates today. Elite E Services USA (Nevada) was established in 2006. EES also has companies and offices in Europe.

About Elite E Services

128

Elite E Services is an electronic boutique brokerage specializing in currency trading, intelligence, and technology surrounding capital markets and electronic trading. EES offers forex trading systems for clients and investors, as well as tools for forex trading. Elite E Services develops and trades FX systems and FX trading technology.

Affiliations

- NFA – National Futures Association (NFA) is the industry-wide, self-regulatory organization for the U.S. futures industry. We strive every day to develop rules, programs and services that safeguard market integrity, protect investors and help our Members meet their regulatory responsibilities. NFA ID: 0373609 Click here to go Elite E Services is a registered CTA (Commodities Trading Advisor) with the CFTC and an NFA member.

- FPL – Fix Protocol Consortium member. The Financial Information eXchange (FIX) Protocol is a messaging standard developed specifically for the real-time electronic exchange of securities transactions. FIX is a public-domain specification owned and maintained by FIX Protocol, Ltd. http://www.fixprotocol.org/members/

- ACM – Association for Computing Machinery - ACM is the world's oldest and largest educational and scientific computing society. Since 1947 ACM has provided a vital forum for the exchange of information, ideas, and discoveries. Today, ACM serves a membership of computing professionals and students in more than 100 countries in all areas of industry, academia, and government. http://www.acm.org/

- Sigevo - **SIGEVO** - home of the ACM Special Interest Group on Genetic and Evolutionary Computation. **Predecessor Organization** -- **ISGEC** International Society for Genetic and Evolutionary Computation

- ASP - Association of Shareware Professionals. Since 1987, the ASP has been dedicated to the advancement of shareware, also known as try-before-you-buy software, as an alternative to conventional retail software. Today the ASP is a vibrant organization with hundreds of members around the world working together to improve their businesses and making it easier for computer users to find quality software at reasonable prices.

- Authorized Tradestation Systems Developer

- Microsoft partner and authorized reseller

FCM - Broker

Currently the FXV1 program is available at "FXCM", Forex Capital Markets, LLC. The largest forex dealer member*

NFA ID: 308179 Click here for BASIC NFA ID 0308179

Website: www.fxcm.com

Forex Capital Markets LLC (FXCM) is regulated as a Forex Dealer Member by the National Futures Association. Forex Dealer Members are U.S. registered Futures Commission Merchants that have greater than 35% of revenue from foreign exchange.

As of September 2006, FXCM held in excess of $215 million in customer funds out of a total of over $770 million held by Forex Dealer Members.*

While there are approximately 31 active Forex Dealer Members with liabilities to customers of approximately $795 million, FXCM holds approximately 1 out of every 3 dollars of customer funds held by Forex Dealer Members.

* [Source: **http://www.nfa.futures.org/news/...**]
(FXCM is the FDM referenced in this NFA document as holding in excess of $215 million in customer funds.)

About FXCM

FXCM Group Releases Financial Data: Over $120 Million in Capital FXCM Group has made an unprecedented public release of its balance sheet and invites other firms within the forex industry to follow its example.

Highlights of the (unaudited) balance sheet include the following:

$120,660,927 In Capital (Assets Minus Liabilities)
$98,657,018 In Operating Cash (Excludes Client Funds)

FXCM Group consists of FXCM Holdings LLC, FXCM LLC, Forex Trading LLC, Forex Capital Markets LLC, Forex Capital Markets LTD, FXCM Asia LTD, and FXCM Canada LTD.

[Source: http://www.fxcm.com/company-profile.jsp]

Introducing Broker

Elite E Services must be the Introducing Broker / Referring Party named on the application. Further instructions can be found on the FXV1 website at www.FXv1.com

Forex Bot Limited / Trade Robot

130

Forex Bot Limited is a global leader in innovative software solutions for automated Forex trading. Its unique patent-based technology provides outstanding opportunity in trading Forex. The main concept of the company is integration of different Forex Technical Analysts who use Trade Robot Trading Technology and actively trade Forex market. By joining them to the pool we were able to collect, sort and filter out best possible combinations of trading strategies to different funds and offer them publicly.

Partnership

Forex Bot Limited is the owner of the Trade Robot technology. Elite E Services offers the trading systems (trading signals and portfolios for investors). Trade Robot provides the execution and strategy analytic software tools. Trade Robot receives a percentage of the trading commissions which cover the costs of the technology and its' use.

Principle Risk Factors

Trading foreign exchange on margin carries a high level of risk, and may not be suitable for all investors. The high degree of leverage can work against you as well as for you. Before deciding to invest in foreign exchange you should carefully consider your investment objectives, level of experience, and risk appetite. The possibility exists that you could sustain a loss of some or all of your initial investment and therefore you should not invest money that you cannot afford to lose. You should be aware of all the risks associated with foreign exchange trading, and seek advice from an independent financial advisor if you have any doubts.

PAMM – Percent Allocation Management Module

All accounts are given their appropriate signals, traded together in a PAMM account. Similar but different to a pool, the PAMM allocates trades to each individual but separate client account on a percentage basis.

The PAMM account allows the trading of multiple accounts as if they were one which gives you the best entry/exit prices available. Additionally, the PAMM keeps each client's account records individually so that gains and losses can be distributed on an equal percentage basis such that each client receives the same percentage rate of return regardless of size of account. The PAMM account rolls over each market day at 5:00PM EST distributing gains and losses on a percentage basis to all clients in the PAMM. Any deposits or withdrawals from accounts are made at rollover time each day.

Internet Trading Risks

There are risks associated with utilizing an Internet-based deal execution trading system including, but not limited to, the failure of hardware, software and Internet connection. Since EES does not control signal power, its reception or routing via Internet, configuration of your equipment or reliability of its connection, we cannot be responsible for communication failures, distortions or delays when trading via the Internet. EES employs back-up systems and contingency plans to minimize the possibility of system failure, and trading via telephone is always available.

Market Risks and Online Trading

The trading platform provides sophisticated order entry and tracking of orders. All stop-loss, limit and entry orders are guaranteed against slippage except in extraordinary volatile market conditions. Trading on-line, no matter how convenient or efficient does not necessarily reduce risks associated with currency trading. All quotes and trades are subject to the terms and conditions of the Client Agreement accessible through this website.

Notices

Elite E Services is a newly established company, for the purpose of developing and offering foreign exchange automated systems, and tools to supplement that trading and development. In addition to this EES offers I.T. services to traders, brokers, and investors of the FX markets. EES is not biased against other markets, but we feel forex is the best market for automated trading and day-trading in general.

Because FXV1 is a general FX portfolio based system that can be applied in many different ways, and there is no exact optimal way to trade the system, there is no conflict of interest in who is trading the system with what capital.

EES has no previous litigation, criminal actions, and has not been involved in any arbitration or disputes. Although EES is a newly established company, the partners are pooling many years of field experience in trading and computers.

Unless otherwise noted, all performance data is derived from live account statements. While it is wise to utilize 'backtesting' and other strategy analytics when developing systems, it is not wise to invest large sums of money into strategies that have not been traded live with real money (even if it is a small amount).

Upon request real account statements can be provided. You may be required to provide your full contact detail and sign a Non-Disclosure document.

Although you can close your account at any time, EES recommends keeping your account open for at least 6 months before judging performance. While the style of trading may be short-term, a medium-term view is required to enjoy the benefits of the short-term strategies, as periods of volatility can create short-term drawdowns.

Trading Methodology

Investment Category

Multi-Strategy managed account investment program within the cash foreign exchange markets (FOREX). Multiple, non-correlated automated strategies covering multiple currency pairs are employed simultaneously on client accounts.

Program Objective

The objective of this Managed Account Program is to seek an enhanced rate of capital appreciation with below average volatility through an actively managed blend of computer-generated systematic algorithms. *Since there are no guarantees that this program will meet its investment objectives or not suffer capital loss, this program is not appropriate for investors seeking monthly income or guaranteed returns.*

Trading Methodology

EES attempts to capitalize on the various opportunities that present themselves in the FOREX market using computer generated strategies that include (but may not be limited to) the following:

1. Short Term Momentum (5 minutes to 2 days)

2. Medium Term Momentum (2 days to 10 days)

3. Short and Medium Term Counter-Trend and Trend Exhaustion (1 hour to 10 days)

4. Oscillator Based and Reverse-Oscillator based (Short term)

5. Day Trading and Swing Trading

EES relies on a strong understanding of performance statistics, a thorough review of trade-history track-records, comprehensive back-testing, stress-testing and scenario-testing and an exhaustive due-diligence process to determine proper strategy allocations among the strategies. EES proactively re-allocates and re-distributes strategies as-needed among the various accounts in an effort to provide strong returns and minimal volatility, and EES retains the right to move strategies in and out of any portfolio in order to achieve these objectives.

This is achieved by the use of statistical software, whereby we can analyze a pool of hundreds of strategies, selecting the few which meet or beat stringent criteria.

Non-Optimized Trading Systems Explained

EES does NOT use "computer aided optimization" in the development, testing or maintenance of trading systems used for this program. Only fixed parameter indicators, even if self-adaptive, are incorporated into a specific trading algorithm. Computer aided optimization is a computerized method of testing various systems and formulas on historic data with the request that the computer find the parameters, rules or numbers that would have generated the best performance (in the past) over the sample data set used during a system test. It may sound like a valid concept, but the problem with the practice of "optimization" in dynamic financial markets is that it can lead to unrealistic test results that are very often untenable when used for real-time trading for the future. "Walk-Forward Optimization" which may or may not be used in some of the strategies employed in this program, is a much more realistic way to test for parameters that are more likely to work in the future.

Portfolio Manager (PM) software technology

PM has access to hundreds of mechanically executed Forex strategies that were traded under actual (Broker) and not Hypothetical (Chart) conditions. The mechanical strategies were coded by the mathematicians and experienced traders. The trades history record list goes back to the year 2002. Portfolios can be created based on factors such as profit, risk tolerance, amount of available margin, percent winners, and other factors.

Program Summary

- Strategies used: Fully-Automated, Computer-Generated, Systematic, Multi-Strategy.

- Portfolio: Approximately 5 Strategies trading on 8 major currency pairs consisting of USD-based and Non-Dollar Crosses.

- Management methodology: Blend of select, statistically non-correlated algorithms and proactive money management.

- Long and short strategies: the ability to profit from both up and down markets, regardless of the world's economic environment.

- Trade length-activity level: Depending on the strategy, trades typically last from 30 minutes to approximately 10 days.

- Data interval used in trading: real-time intra-day price-tick data.

- Non Optimized: Only fixed parameter indicators are incorporated into this algorithm--no computer aided optimization.

- Money management: Position sizing relative to account sizing with max drawdown protection and per trade stop loss management.

- Maximum leverage per account: Leverage for each strategy may range from .5 to 1 (IE: No Leverage used) to 20 to 1 (20 Times Leverage). Although leverage-used constantly fluctuates in each account from hour to hour, The average leverage used relative to account size is approximately 4.5 to 1.

- Liquidity: Anyday, if terminating or withdrawing. Otherwise, additions are possible on the first (1st) and the fifteenth (15th) of each month.

Manager compensation:

- Management Fee: Accounts are assessed a Two Percent (2%) annual management fee (paid monthly).

- Performance incentive fee: A Twenty Percent (25%) performance incentive fee on net new profits above a high-water mark.

- Execution cost assumptions: Our spot forex transactions have $15 per 100k traded commission (per round turn). This fee covers the technology involved in execution.

- Minimum account size generally required to begin trading: $10,000 USD or USD equivalent. *EES strongly recommends you invest for at least one year before fairly evaluating EES's performance. Therefore, you should commit to retain the investment for a minimum of one year to fully realize the potential of this program. However, if you so choose, you can close your account at any time.*

The Trading System

The strategies are designed and provided by experienced traders and mathematicians from all over the world. Each Strategy Provider has passed through the strict testing procedure and is forced to use Trade Robot™ Trading Technology to be qualified for strategy provider pool. Using TRT Technology means that any trade presented at our pages was executed by the broker and are not there as result of back testing inside the charting program. The main importance of TRTT principle is that Trade Robot™ records trades in real time and protect it from any possibility to manipulate on it. It means that data collected by Trade Robot™ are audited, accurate and transparent.

Over the past several years we have collected results from thousand of different strategies and diligently recorded it. By use of special designed computer program we have composed them into the Forex Spot Funds that are listed at our pages.

All the funds are managed by use of Trade Robot™ Trading Technology that means trades and accounts are managed automated and without human involvement. Funds are monitored by group of well educated computer experts who take care about overall technical stability.

We believe that coding the trading rules in trading strategy and leave it to be executed by the Trade Robots™ drastically increase the probability of trading profitable. We further believe that composing different strategies by use of different currency pairs, time frames and different analytic ideas additionally increase probability of trading profitable. Excluding the human as an emotional reacting being is of essential importance for successful trading. By use of such principles we are able for the first time to compare such funds with Mutual, Hedge or any other traditional funds.

About Fund principles and investing procedure

Common characteristic for any listed fund is ultimate transparency and simplicity for investors:

- Trading portfolio is composed with variety of currency pairs from different Strategy Developers approved through strict rules created by Trade Robots™ technology

- Trades are executed automatically by use of Trade Robots™

- Investors accounts are updated automatically each trading day

- Calculation of individual assets are based on Mutual Fund principle by use of NAV (Net Asset Value)

- Investor is able to access his trading account any time from

136

anywhere

- Investor is able to withdraw money from his account in any time from anywhere by simple press on button

- Investor is able to upload money by simple administration process

- Investor is able to switch money to any listed fund by simple press on button

- Investor is able to compose fund of funds, allocate provisional investment and simulate its performance. After being satisfy with results by simple press on button it can be easily initiate registration.

About Trade Robot Technology

Trade Robot Limited introduces the FX Trade Robot® a fully automated order execution system for the Forex market that will place your Trading system's signals, or one of our System Provider's signals directly into your dealing station and then manages your trades. Developed by traders for traders, the FX Trade Robot was developed to overcome the human limitations of systematic trade execution such as fear, greed, fatigue, and the psychological factors that affect traders during trading.
In addition, it has the ability to execute trades in multiple markets and on multiple strategies that would be physically impossible for even a large group of traders to accomplish. Now traders with or without trading systems can take advantage of the benefits of trading with the FX Trade Robot.

Risk Management

Dynamic and self adjusted risk control:

Most trades are executed electronically via an automated platform and automatically "micro managed" using dynamically self-adjusting risk control measures that generate initial stop-loss, trailing stops and profit targets based on their individual volatility characteristics. Typically, there are three risk-management strategies used:

- **Initial protective stop loss**— to mitigate market exposure risk,

- **Trailing stop--** to reduced trade exposure and lock in profitable trades,

- **Profit target**—to attempt to capitalize on rapid or abnormal moves that might not otherwise be realized due to rapid market changes. These quick market moves are usually the result of unexpected news events.

How risk control and profit objectives work

At the same time an original entry trade-signal is issued, an initial protective stop-loss order is also issued. Once a position is opened, the initial protective stop loss helps limit market risk. If a trade moves in the anticipated direction by a certain amount, a trailing stop order is generated that takes over from the initial protective stop-loss order and follows the price action to further reduce potential losses. If the market's direction continues, then the trailing stop begins to lock in market profits. If the market makes a rapid or abnormal move in the correct direction or just a smoothed sustained move, a profit target may be reached. Conversely, if a market does not move in the anticipated direction, the position will be stopped-out with a loss, as is typical in trading markets.

Money management—Position Sizing

Professional traders and money managers often consider sound money management and position-sizing methodology to be the single most important aspect of a successful investment program. The position-sizing strategy employed by each sub-advisor in the program uses a three-tiered money management overlay that adjusts trade position size based on equity growth, market volatility and system performance in order to either increase profit potential or reduce market risk exposure as appropriate. Position sizing, though important, is used with discretion as much of the 'hedge' against adverse markets comes from the proper diversification among strategies.

EES's Efforts to reduce volatility

Reducing volatility and protecting profits when trends quickly reverse is a phenomenon that purely trend-following or discretionary money managers

138

sometimes have problems with. EES has attempted to deal with this issue by combining strategies and systems that use short term and medium term term horizons together. For the most part, strategies that employ long-term horizons are avoided because they tend to contribute undue additional risk and volatility of returns. As a counterbalance, an additional layer of safety through diversification is sought through the blend of various non-correlated strategies. However, there is no guarantee that this effort alone will continue to be the case or that losses can be prevented.

IMPORTANT NOTE ON TRADE EXECUTION POLICY

EES aims to rely on the automated computer-generated trading signals for trading in customer accounts. However, if determined necessary at any time, EES reserves the right to intervene in the trading and/or trade execution process during periods of, for example but not limited to, extreme volatility, unduly low liquidity or any other aberrant market conditions. Intervention may take the form of adjusting position size, system parameters, preventing trades from being executed, or any other overriding of computerized system algorithms. Any such action would be taken primarily for the purposes of risk-reduction and not necessarily for profit-enhancement. Preservation of capital is our primary concern. Such action taken by EES may be taken without prior notification to the client.

Links and references

Elite E Services USA Homepage: http://www.eliteeservices.net

National Futures Association: http://nfa.futures.org

FXV1 Homepage: http://www.FXv1.com

Joe Gelet NFA: nfa ID 0364715

Elite E Services NFA: nfa ID 0373609

Performance Data

Automated Currency Managed Accounts using Proprietary Portfolio Management (PPM)

Using EES proprietary PPM software, a portfolio can be created that is comprised of a mix of balanced system on a range of currency pairs. PPM has access to hundreds of mechanically executed Forex strategies that were traded under actual (Broker) and not Hypothetical (Chart) conditions. The mechanical strategies were coded by the mathematicians and experienced traders. The trades' history record list goes back to the year 2002.

Using PPM, it is possible to create a strategy which is a 'super strategy' comprised of hundreds of systems. Some of the systems may only trade once a week or once a month. However when you combine all of them you have a day trading system that trades on multiple pairs. It is a 'basket of systems' that comprise a portfolio of automated forex trading systems.

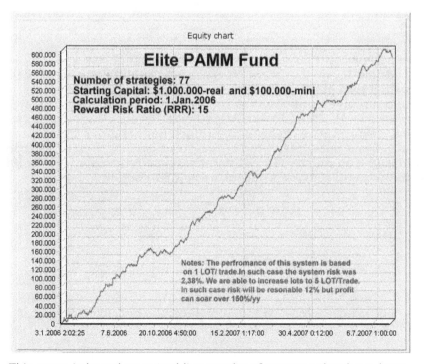

This curve is based on actual live results of systems that have been

140

sending signals to the systems database over the past several years. That means, this is the account balance if these systems have been traded. There are accounts which have traded these systems, referenced below.

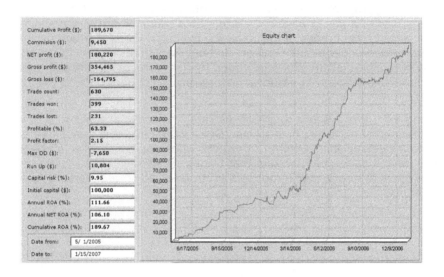

Cumulative Profit ($):	189,670
Commision ($):	9,450
NET profit ($):	180,220
Gross profit ($):	354,465
Gross loss ($):	-164,795
Trade count:	630
Trades won:	399
Trades lost:	231
Profitable (%):	63.33
Profit factor:	2.15
Max DD ($):	-7,650
Run Up ($):	10,804
Capital risk (%):	9.95
Initial capital ($):	100,000
Annual ROA (%):	111.66
Annual NET ROA (%):	106.10
Cumulative ROA (%):	189.67
Date from:	5/ 1/2005
Date to:	1/15/2007

Trading Foreign Exchange carries a high level of risk and may not be suitable for all investors. There is a possibility that you could sustain a loss of all or more of your investment therefore you should not invest money that you cannot afford to lose. You should be aware of all the risks associated with Foreign Exchange trading. If this performance report and/or document is older than 6 months from today's date, (as dated on the front cover), then this report is outdated; you must contact the representative who gave you this document and request a recently updated version.

What are the results?

The target of systems is to achieve on average 10% per month with medium leverage.   Note the difference in the above chart and the below. The above chart is a hypothetical portfolio built on live actual results. That means using actual trades from the past several years, a portfolio is built. The below chart is a live account statement.

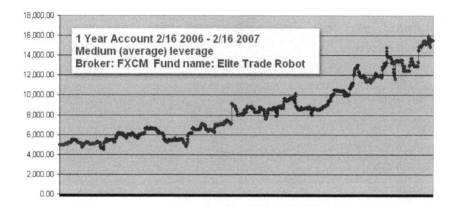

This above graph is based on a **live account statement** using the portfolio approach. It is summarized in the performance table below:

Trading Commission		-1,308.00
Interest Fee		-51.21
Profit/Loss of Trade		**9,791.98**
Deposit		11,924.00
Withdrawal		0
Funds transfer		-3,500.00
Options Payout		0
Options Commission		0
Withdrawal Fee		0
Management Fee		0
Performance Fee		-1,390.04
Deposit Rollback		0
Ending Balance		15,466.73
Floating P/L		285.58
Equity		15,752.31
Necessary Margin		4,200.00
Usable Margin		11,552.31

The above numbers represent a live account statement gaining 82% after fees in 1 year. There are accounts which have outperformed the above, which is due to higher leverage setting. There are accounts which also have performed less than the above, but there are no accounts which are negative from open, using this technology.

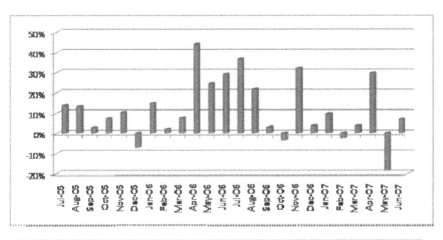

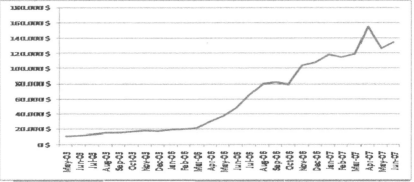

Individual account statements may vary, due to leverage settings and other factors. The above graphs are based on real trading history, not hypothetical backtesting.

Client Manual

All requests regarding the trading of your account should be directed to Elite E Services at:

www.eliteeservices.net

info@eliteeservices.net

646-837-0059

Any request involving deposit and withdrawl, or any other account related question should be directed to fxcm at:

Contact FXCM - Client Support Information

Product Inquiries and Service Numbers

FXCM representatives are available 24 hours a day, 7 days a week.

Toll-Free US Sales: +1 888 50 FOREX (36739)

Sales and Client Services: +1 212 201 7301

Technical Support: +1 212 201 7302

Live Operator: +1 212 897 7660

Fax (US): +1 877 229 0004

Fax (US and International): +1 212 897 7669

E-mail: info@fxcm.com

FXCM Account access provided at:

https://www.myfxcm.com/

Depositing Funds:

http://www.fxcm.com/depositing-funds.jsp

Open your account online:

www.fxv1.com

Be sure to name Elite E Services as the Introducing Broker on your account application.

Appendix A

Possible causes of unintended consequences include the world's inherent complexity (parts of a system responding to changes in the environment), perverse incentives, human stupidity, self-deception or other cognitive or emotional biases.

Robert K. Merton listed five causes of unanticipated consequences:

1.   *Ignorance* (It is impossible to anticipate everything)
2.   *Error* (Incomplete analysis of the problem, or following habits that worked in the past but may not apply to the current situation)
3.   *Immediate interest* which may override long-term interests
4.   *Basic values* may require or prohibit certain actions, even if the long-term result might be unfavorable (these long-term consequences may eventually cause changes in basic values)
5.   *Self-defeating prophecy* (Fear of some consequence drives people to find solutions before the problem occurs, thus the non-occurrence of the problem is unanticipated)

Interest rate swap

From Wikipedia, the free encyclopedia

In the field of derivatives, a popular form of swap is the **interest rate swap**, in which one party exchanges a stream of interest for another party's stream. Interest rate swaps are normally 'fixed against floating', but can also be 'fixed against fixed' or 'floating against floating' rate swaps. Interest rate swaps are often used by companies to re-allocate their exposure to interest-rate fluctuations, typically by exchanging fixed-rate obligations for floating rate obligations.

Valuation and Pricing

The present value of a plain vanilla (i.e. straightforward) swap can easily be computed using standard methods of determining the present value of the components. The swap requires from one party a series of payments based on variable rates, which are determined at the agreed dates of each payment. At the time the swap is entered into, only the actual payment rates of the fixed leg are known in the future, but an estimation of the future rates of the floating leg are derived from the yield curve: the yield of bonds with various maturity dates stretching from the short term to the long term. Each variable rate payment is calculated based on the forward rate for each respective payment date. Using these interest rates leads to a series of cash flows. Each cash flow is discounted by the zero-coupon rate for the date of the payment; this is also sourced from the yield curve data available from the market. Zero-coupon rates are used because these rates are for bonds which pay only one cash flow. The interest rate swap is therefore treated like a series of zero-coupon bonds.

This calculation leads to a PV. The fixed rate offered in the swap is the rate which values the fixed rates payments at the same PV as the variable rate payments using today's forward rates. Therefore, at the time the contract is entered into, there is no advantage to either party, and therefore the swap requires no upfront payment. During the life of the swap, the same valuation technique is used, but since, over time, the forward rates change, the PV of the variable-rate part of the swap will deviate from the unchangeable fixed-rate side of the swap. Therefore, the swap will be an asset to one party and a liability to the other. The way these changes in value are reported is the subject of IAS 39 for jurisdictions following IFRS.

Marking to Market

The current valuation of securities in a portfolio. Debt Security Traders mostly use this in order to visualize their inventory at a certain time.

Fannie Mae

Fannie Mae uses interest rate derivatives to for example "hedge" its cash flow. The products it uses are pay-fixed swaps, receive-fixed swaps, basis swaps, interest rate cap and swaptions, and forward starting swaps. Its "cash flow hedges" had a notional value of $872 billion at December 31, 2003, while its "fair value hedges" stood ˣat $169 billion (SEC Filings) (2003 10-K page 79). Its "net value" on "a net present value basis, to settle at current market rates all outstanding derivative contracts" was (7,712) million and 8,139 million, which makes a total of 6,633 million when a "purchased options time value" of 8,139 million is added.

What Fannie Mae doesn't want is for example a wide "duration gap" for a long period. If rates turn the opposite way on a duration gap the cash flow from assets and liabilities may not match, resulting in inability to pay the bills on liabilities. It reports the duration gap regularly in its (8-K Regulation FD Disclosure), see earlier 10-K's for charts and more information (Investor Relations: Annual Reports & Proxy Statements). (Dec 1999 - Dec 2002 duration gap) , (2003 gap).

REFERENCES

ⁱ (See Breton Woods)
ⁱⁱ www.fxcyberschool.com

ⁱⁱⁱ Global Correlations in Random Data

   The Global Consciousness Project, also called the EGG Project, is an international and multidisciplinary collaboration of scientists, engineers, artists and others. This website introduces methods and technology and empirical results in one section, and presents interpretations and applications in another.

 We have been collecting data from a global network of random event generators since August, 1998. The network has grown to about 65 host sites around the world running custom software that reads the output of physical random number generators and records a 200-bit trial sum once every second, continuously over months and years. The data are transmitted over the internet to a server in Princeton, NJ, USA, where they are archived for later analysis. Individual data create a tapestry of color. The dot below shows coherence.

   The purpose of this project is to examine subtle correlations that appear to reflect the presence and activity of consciousness in the world. The scientific work is careful, but it is at the margins of our understanding. We believe our view may be enriched by a creative and poetic perspective. Here we present various aspects of the project, including some insight into its scientific and philosophical implications.

[http://noosphere.princeton.edu/]

^{iv} **Unintended consequences** are situations where an action results in an outcome that is not (or not only) what is intended. The unintended results may be foreseen or unforeseen, but they should be the logical or likely results of the action. For example, it is often conjectured that if the Treaty of Versailles had not imposed such harsh conditions on Germany, World War II would not have occurred. From this perspective, war could be considered an unintended consequence of the Treaty of Versailles.

Unintended consequences can be classed into roughly three types:

- a positive unexpected benefit, usually referred to as serendipity or a windfall
- a potential source of problems, according to Murphy's law used in Systems engineering
- a negative or a perverse effect, which is the opposite result of what is intended

Discussions of unintended consequences usually refer to the third situation of perverse results. This situation often arises because a policy has a Perverse incentive and causes actions contrary to what is desired.

[v] Meta Trader www.metaquotes.net
- Download client terminal (3Mb) and open demo-account
- Read User Guide

[vi] http://currencytradingcharts.com/

[vii] [http://FXtrade.oanda.com/FXtrade/api/index.shtml]

[viii] [http://www.nondealingdesk.blogspot.com/]

[ix] [http://en.wikipedia.org/wiki/Money]